Visions of the Apocalypse

Receptions of John's Revelation in Western Imagination

Bruce Chilton

BAYLOR UNIVERSITY PRESS

Cover design by Kara Davison, Faceout Studio.
Images ©Shutterstock/Ohmega 1982, Stella Caraman, Canicula

Library of Congress Cataloging-in-Publication Data

Chilton, Bruce.
Visions of the Apocalypse : receptions of John's revelation in western imagination / Bruce Chilton.
175 pages cm
Includes bibliographical references and index.
ISBN 978-1-60258-982-7 (pbk. : alk. paper)
1. Bible. Revelation—Criticism, interpretation, etc. I. Title.
BS2825.52.C48 2013
228'.0609--dc23
2013007944

Printed in the United States of America on acid-free paper with a minimum of 30% post-consumer waste recycled content.

Contents

Acknowledgments

Students at Bard College have prompted me over the years to grapple with the Apocalypse. Interacting with them has made me see that the most important issue in teaching is often not what John of Patmos says, but what has been said about John to influence my students before they even open his book.

For that reason, this textbook first of all addresses the history of interpretation relating to the Revelation of John, although with reference to specific passages that are crucial to that rich story of conflicting claims. The close of the study then deals with the structure of the Apocalypse, so that any reader can see how the text is designed internally, where it relates to the types of interpretation discussed from the outset, and what meanings can be derived from John's mysterious work and its long history of interpretation.

Much of this book was written while I served as visiting professor at the Chinese University of Hong Kong. The colleagues, students, and facilities I enjoyed supported me on many levels; Professors Lung Kwon Lo and Eric Wong provided a rich and invaluable experience.

When it came to framing the work for publication, the design of dealing with the reception history as well as the structure of the Apocalypse proved a challenge. But given what students face when they approach the work, that challenge had to be met. In attempting to do that, the editorial expertise of Carey Newman proved crucial. He and his staff at Baylor University Press have offered substantive help as well as encouragement.

B. D. C.
Annandale-on-Hudson

Introduction

When you open the Revelation of John, what do you expect to read?

Millions of people today approach the last book in the Bible as a literal guide to the end of the world. But for more than a hundred years, many educated readers, including Christians and skeptics, have rejected John's violent images and appeals for divine vengeance; George Bernard Shaw even called the text "the curious record of the visions of a drug addict."[1] Yet Augustine of Hippo saw in the Apocalypse neither predictions of catastrophe nor irrational fantasies, but a symbolic representation of the new age of faith that had dawned with Christ's coming.

A wide variety of readings (only sampled in the last paragraph) have prompted studies that make sense of how successive generations have responded to the text. Approaches of that kind are usually called "reception history," but the Revelation of John involves several histories of its interpretation. At a deeper level, the story of how the Apocalypse has been understood goes beyond scholarly interest. Readers often bring to the text pre-understandings that control how they will interpret its words, and those assumptions reflect how they see the shape of human destiny. Deep convictions are often involved, not merely working hypotheses of what the book means.

Readers naturally come to the reading of any text with expectations of what it is going to mean and how it might affect them. Factors such as how a book is marketed, and whether it forms part of the Bible, influence our judgment of the significance it is likely to have. In the case of the Revelation of John, however, the powerful expectations of what the text is going to mean, before it is even encountered, have often proven uniquely influential—even determinative—within readers' interpretations.

The purpose of this textbook is to enable readers to engage with the Revelation of John. Experience has shown me that the usual advice that teachers of the Bible give their students—to leave one's presuppositions behind and confront the Scriptures anew—is inadequate in this case. To deal with the Apocalypse, we need to be aware from an early stage of how the book has been understood, because those understandings have produced programs of interpretation that have influenced generations of readers whether or not they are aware of that influence. It is *not* my purpose to dismiss any of these interpretations, but to explain how they arose as understandings of the text. On that basis, we will move on in the last chapter to deal with the Apocalypse as the source that has produced diverse readings because it confronts readers with the challenge of processing religious visions.

Even the book's title makes for disagreement. Should we say *Revelation* or *Apocalypse* of John? In common English, each word travels in a different circle of meaning. "Apocalypse" typically relates to the end of the world—the final judgment with its cataclysmic sequence of destruction, famine, and fire—while "revelation" might speak of what is disclosed to a seer, insight into divine realities that are inherently timeless.

The dichotomy between "revelation" and "apocalypse" in English to some extent reflects the happenstance of translation. Both words derive from similar meanings and etymologies in their respective languages. Greek *apokalupsis* and Latin *revelatio* refer to a "cover" (a Greek *kalupsis* or a Latin *velatio*) that has been removed (Greek *apo-* or Latin *re-*). The divergence of English meanings between apocalypse and revelation illustrates how the usage of a word shapes its significance more than its linguistic origin. English speakers think of cataclysm as apocalyptic and of insight as revelatory and bring those associations to the book they call either the Revelation or the Apocalypse.

Yet this division of meaning also conveys the character of John of Patmos' book, the source not only of both words in English but of ample material to support reading it as an apocalyptic scenario *and* as an existential moment of timeless revelation. The Revelation of John gives us paradigms of "apocalypse" and "revelation." How readers understand those paradigms in turn influences, and in some cases has determined, how people view the text.

Prophecies of the end of the world have often been grounded in the Revelation of John, and chapter 6 of this textbook analyzes the modern emphasis on apocalyptic catastrophe. But an earlier prophetic reading of the Apocalypse, from the second century, looked forward to a thousand years of *bliss* (chapter 1), not disaster. Both views are "millennial," concerned with the final thousand years of history, and yet they differ as much in their views of the end of humanity as they do in emotional tone. Both ancient millennialism and modern millennialism seek to write histories of the future, but their findings are profoundly different.

Alongside that controversy an even more fundamental disagreement has made interpretation of the Apocalypse contentious. A large body of thought, which dominated commentary on the Revelation for nearly a thousand years, saw the text as a symbolic reflection of eternity, not a timetable for the end of the world.

The Apocalypse *Millenarian Prophecy or Symbolic Insight?*

As early as the third century, Origen of Alexandria insisted that, instead of prophesying history and its end, the Apocalypse refers to an "eternal gospel" (Rev 14:6). That phrase signals a new, spiritual understanding of Christ, "the realities of which his actions were symbols" (*Commentary on John* 1.39-40). Origen saw the Apocalypse as the symbolic key to how God is revealed in all time. His approach influenced major thinkers in the early church (chapter 2).

The Augustinian interpretation, a great and enduring tradition grounded in the approach of Origen, plumbed the liturgical dimension of the Apocalypse. The Revelation's visions depict worship in heaven itself and invite those who hear the text to become worshippers themselves, to join in the songs and music of angelic choruses, in effect to enter heaven for the purpose of divine praise. That transition from earth to heaven, a basic move within the gnostic strategy of antiquity and the traditions it drew upon, made the text a vertical journey through space rather than a horizontal journey across time, and provided the sense that the community at worship embodied heaven in the midst of the world. God endowed his people with the supernatural riches and authority necessary for the world's health—by violent means, Augustine taught, if necessary.

Both the predictive paradigm and the symbolic paradigm have thrived in interpretation. They unfolded throughout history but also have vigorous representatives now. Yet there is no getting around the fact that the second type of interpretation refutes the first, seeing in the Revelation's millennium (Rev 20:4-5) a symbol of the mystical rule of the church, and not a thousand years of actual rule on earth.

These and other battles have brought with them, not only trenchant disputes over the meaning of the text, but also rhetorical assaults on the character of interpreters. To this day, millenarians are often dismissed as crude literalists, while their opponents are accused of denying the millennium altogether with their symbolic interpretations. In chapters 1 and 2, we will see that those accusations are unfounded: both the millennial and the symbolic interpretations have grappled with the Apocalypse as a text and as a guide to human destiny.

The two stances toward interpreting the Revelation in the first four centuries of its life, the millenarian and the symbolic, stood behind controversies concerning its place in the canon. Issues of authorship and date were often cited, but they sometimes appear to be surrogates for one interpretative orientation or the other.

Canonical Controversies

The Revelation's uncertain authorship meant that it made its way into the canon by way of controversy. No other work in the

New Testament had quite the difficulty that the Revelation did in acquiring canonical status.

Reference to the Apocalypse by Christian teachers during the second century was enthusiastic. Irenaeus, writing from Gaul, claimed that it was written by John the apostle (and author of the Fourth Gospel), although very late in a long life. Irenaeus' dedication to the book was rooted in his conviction that it correctly depicted the new Jerusalem (Rev 21:2), not in any allegorical sense, but as a real reign of the saints (*Against Heresies* 5.35). Irenaeus had come from Asia Minor, as had Papias and Melito of Sardis, second-century teachers who also embraced the book with an enthusiastic millennialism. Justin Martyr came from Samaria, but spent time in Ephesus before settling in Rome, where he championed the idea of the Revelation's apostolic authorship as well as millennialism. In North Africa, Tertullian joined the company of these enthusiasts (as discussed in chapter 1).

Enthusiasm for prophecy grounded in the Apocalypse led to a forceful counter-reaction. Tertullian himself became a Montanist in later life; Montanism was a movement inspired by the practice of what was styled "new prophecy." Montanus claimed the authority of both John's Gospel, with its promise of "another comforter" (John 14:16) and the new Jerusalem of the Apocalypse. During the second century, Christian teachers outside of Asia Minor largely turned away from claims of prophecy (new or otherwise) in favor of more settled models of authority; some of them claimed that neither the Gospel of John nor the Apocalypse should be accepted as apostolic or canonical.

Two factors made the balance of criticism tip more against the Apocalypse than the Fourth Gospel. First, the Gospel's evidently analogical language, which made it a "spiritual Gospel" in the famous phrase of Clement of Alexandria (cited by Eusebius, *History of the Church* 6.14.5-7), distanced it from the militant stance associated with Montanism. Second, the language and style of the Apocalypse differ from the Gospel's, and its visionary content is easily applied in the interests of millenarianism, Montanist or otherwise.

During the third century CE, Dionysius, bishop of Alexandria, showed by critical analysis that the Revelation was not written by the author of the Fourth Gospel. The purpose of his argument was not merely to adjudicate the question of authorship. His methods have often met with scholarly approval during the modern period, and they made a considerable contribution to the study of the Revelation and the Gospel according to John, but Dionysius' overall goal went beyond issues of history.

Dionysius' criticism of the authorship of the Apocalypse raised doubts in relation to its place in the canon, especially in the eastern, Greek-speaking church. But as a result of the influence of Athanasius of Alexandria (297–373 CE), a dominant bishop in the history of the church, the place of the Revelation was secured. Athanasius was the champion of what became Orthodox Christology, the view that Jesus as the Son of God should be seen as of one essence (*ousia*) with the Father. The visions in the Apocalypse of the Lamb being worshipped with God in heaven (see, e.g., Rev 5:13) supported his view, and at the same time, the theme of resistance in the book shows that the more Christ was rejected, the greater faithful witness to his truth among the martyrs became.

When Athanasius listed the books in the canon of Scripture, he even paraphrased Revelation 22:18-19, "Let no one add to these; let nothing be taken away from them" (*Thirty-Ninth Festal Letter* 6). The book seemed to show both the way to orthodoxy with its claim of the transcendent truth of the Trinity and the need to resist orthodoxy's enemies. So the Revelation was embraced as canonical, but as symbolic theology rather than literal prophecy.

Types of Interpretation

Depending upon the period, the Revelation has been seen as the direct prophecy of a thousand-year reign by Christ's followers (the millennial interpretation, from the second century) or as announcing the already accomplished spiritual dominion of the church (the symbolic interpretation, from the fourth century). But these deeply opposed approaches are by no means the only types of interpretation that have claimed to explain the Apocalypse.

From the twelfth century, the Revelation was treated as an oracular source that signaled supernatural change on earth caused by the coming of the antichrist. The term *antichristos* never appears in the Apocalypse; the New Testament uses the term elsewhere, but provides little description. John of Patmos' vision of the great red dragon with seven heads (Rev 12:3-10, 17:7-11) was held during the Middle Ages to fill in that *lacuna*, and to provide the key to history (chapter 3). The conviction that the antichrist could be identified by means of the Apocalypse and encountered in battle on earth in the supernatural war that had spilled out of heaven, became a powerful source of revolutionary zeal during the sixteenth century (chapter 4).

Against the view that the antichrist was apparent in the battles of the Reformation, an approach known as "preterism" developed, in which the prophecies of the Revelation are held to have been fulfilled in the ancient past. Just as there are millenarians today who contend against those who read the Revelation symbolically, so there are preterists who dispute claims that the text finds its completion in our time, since they believe it relates only to the past. Histories of interpretation have been written that attempt to class *all* commentaries into the camps of millenarians and their opponents, or of preterists and their opponents. But the life of the book proves more complex than a single opposition of that sort can capture; controversies belong within their periods, and should not be globalized to subsume the interests of other types of interpretation.

The Enlightenment's signature concern for progress in reading the Revelation turned the Apocalypse into an agenda of social, religious, and even scientific reform during the eighteenth century. As we will see in chapter 5, great social movements such as the opposition to slavery were motivated by this interpretation, but it also proves crucial in understanding the Great Awakening associated with Jonathan Edwards, and even the scientific confidence of Sir Isaac Newton.

Yet as early as the nineteenth century, and cresting during the twentieth century, a new millennialism emerged. Unlike its ancient counterpart, however, the modern version read the

Apocalypse as a chronological map of catastrophe, from which believers would be saved by the "rapture" (chapter 6). This concept is even less present in the Revelation than the antichrist is, and appears somewhat allusively in only one New Testament passage (1 Thess 4:17), but it has governed the approach of a great deal of exegesis.

These types of interpretation all have lives of their own; none of them has died out, and each has adherents today. Their relationship to one another, and the power of their readings, will concern us as we trace their influence in the chapters that follow. But in no case are these interpretations merely exegetical possibilities; rather, they have motivated people to live their lives, and sometimes to confront their deaths, in the light of what the Revelation told them about their destiny. Although major interpreters will be discussed in relation to each type of interpretation, in no case can a type be viewed as the creation of a single person. Rather, the thinkers we will meet investigated the text in terms of sensibilities in deep sympathy with the orientations of their periods. Other representatives from each type might have been chosen, but those mentioned here remain prominent in critical discussion. Waves of interpretation have pushed the overall sense of the Revelation in differing directions over time. These patterns of meaning have emanated both directly from the text and from around the text, so that the relationship between the book and its environment needs to be appreciated, if its impact is to be understood.

Understanding John of Patmos Today

When views of a text vary widely, it is tempting to suppose that the interpretation involved is arbitrary. In fact, however, each of the types of interpretation we trace develops from a detailed consideration of dimensions of meaning found within the Revelation of John. For that reason, at the head of each chapter a passage appears that particularly encourages the type of interpretation under discussion, although many other passages are considered within the course of each chapter.[2]

Readings of the Apocalypse that predicted millennial catastrophe prompted a counterreaction during the twentieth century, like George Bernard Shaw's. The popular appeal of the rapture and cataclysmic interpretations also caused some scholars to take up a skeptical stance toward the book. Mainline churches today incorporate only brief passages of the Revelation within their worship, usually laundering them of their apocalyptic dimension.

During the twentieth century, anti-Semitism was a beneficiary of sidelining the Apocalypse. The great novelist D. H. Lawrence wrote a book on the Revelation in which he claimed that all apocalyptic literature was an exercise in compensation, in which the Jews lost their land and fantasized an alternative reality. The Revelation allegedly belongs to this class of literature, seeking to give the powerless an imaginary taste of revenge against the powerful. Often, the Apocalypse has been dismissed as more "Jewish" than "Christian." More recently, scholars have made a coherent case for seeing the Apocalypse apart from preconceived distinctions of that kind. John of Patmos did not use the term "Christianity" any more than Paul, and John's claim to the inheritance of Israel was no less vociferous than Paul's.

With this new openness to the Revelation as a religious text without preconceived boundaries, promising developments have emerged in interpretation. During most periods in the life of the Revelation, apocalyptic thinking has been the common property of popular devotion and critical reflection. Tensions between those uses arise naturally, but mutual rejection is by no means necessary. Conservative Evangelicals affirm the future dimension of the Revelation's meaning, while many others question the human capacity to know that future in detail. Liberal scholars have argued that John's language was never intended to be literal, and have revived a symbolic approach to the text, although without Augustine's triumphalism. Differences that once seemed hard-edged are allowing for much more nuance than was once the case.

Yet even as criticisms of literalism have been developed, the appeal of a realized Armageddon, the battle described in Revelation 16:16, has proven durable. That final war—as well as the destruction of Gog and Magog (Rev 20:8-9) and many other images from the Apocalypse—today features not only in popular Christian predictions of final catastrophe, but also in a form of Judaism which is calling for a triumphant Third Temple to be built in Zion and in Islamist calls for dedicated *jihad.* The urgency of coping with literally militaristic readings of the Apocalypse—Christian, Jewish, and Muslim—has never been greater, because they have been incorporated into some of the most violent movements of our time.

John of Patmos took evident pride in his achievement, yet his book is as puzzling as it has proven influential. For two thousand years, readers, whether in sympathy or opposition from within the Christian tradition or from quite different perspectives, have tried to understand what the book's visions mean. All these attempts show us something about the Revelation and about how people have conceived the fate of human beings. None of them can yet claim supremacy, although the conclusion at the end of this book suggests strategies for reading the Revelation with an awareness of its lives since it was written.

Further Reading

The interface between the Apocalypse and interpretation is explored in John M. Court, *Myth and History in the Book of Revelation* (London: SPCK, 1979); Gerhard Maier, *Die Johannesoffenbarung und die Kirche*, Wissenschaftliche Untersuchungen zum Neuen Testament 25 (Tübingen: Mohr, 1981); and Richard B. Hays and Stefan Alkier, eds., *Revelation and the Politics of Apocalyptic Interpretation* (Waco, Tex.: Baylor University Press, 2012).

In the cases of Eusebius, Augustine, and many patristic authors, useful translations and editions are available in the Loeb Classical Library of Harvard University Press (here adapted). Origen is not well represented in that collection, and the editorial state of his work is far from straightforward; as an alternative, see Origen, *Commentary on the Gospel According to John* 1, Fathers of the Church 80, trans. Ronald E. Heine (Washington, D.C.: Catholic University of America, 1989). See also Irenaeus, *Against Heresies,* trans. Alexander Roberts, James Donaldson, and A. Cleveland Coxe in

Ante-Nicene Fathers (Peabody: Hendrickson, 1994); and E. P. Meijering, ed. and trans., *Athanasius: De Incarnatione Verbi, Einleitung, Übersetzung, Kommentar,* with J. C. N. van Winden (Amsterdam: Gieben, 1989).

The typological approach of this study is inspired by Max Weber. See Edward A. Shils and Henry A. Finch, eds. and trans., *Max Weber on the Methodology of the Social Sciences* (Glencoe, Ill.: Free Press, 1949).

On some of the diverse appropriation of the Revelation mentioned here, see Mara Kalnins, ed., *Apocalypse and the Writings on Revelation: The Cambridge Edition of the Works of D. H. Lawrence* (Cambridge: Cambridge University Press, 2002); John W. Marshall, *Parables of War: Reading John's Jewish Apocalypse*, Studies in Christianity and Judaism 10 (Waterloo, Ont.: Wilfred Laurier University Press, 2001); Motti Inbari, *Jewish Fundamentalism and the Temple Mount: Who Will Build the Third Temple?* trans. Shaul Vardi (Albany: State University of New York Press, 2009); and Jean-Pierre Filiu, *Apocalypse in Islam*, trans. M. B. DeBevoise (Berkeley: University of California Press, 2011).

1

A Thousand Years of Joy

> And I saw an angel coming down from heaven having the key of the abyss and a great chain in his hand. And he seized the dragon, the primordial serpent who is the devil and Satan, and bound him for a thousand years and threw him into the abyss and closed and sealed it over him, that he might not still deceive the nations until the thousand years have been completed. After this he must be loosed for a small period.
>
> Revelation 20:1-3

The millennium, the thousand years referred to here in the Revelation of John, became a standard way in the West to speak of the ultimate future of humanity. In today's popular culture millennial expectations are typically laced with horror, threat, and the dread of cataclysm. A long-running series called Left Behind includes best-selling books and widely distributed films, and has popularized a reading of the Revelation as the planet's deathwatch. Feature-film releases such as *Melancholia* (2011) and *Seeking a Friend for the End of the World* (2012) appropriate the language of the Revelation and apply it to their own scenarios of catastrophe.[1] It is fascinating to see how and why recent interpretations have come to see the Revelation of John in terms of unrelieved disaster. But that is a story for a later chapter. To understand the impact of the Apocalypse, we need to begin at the beginning. During the century after the book was written, the millennium emerged as a principle of hope, rather than as a prediction of disaster.

The Revelation promises a thousand years, not of catastrophe, but of utopian righteousness and enjoyment. John of Patmos says in chapter 20 that he saw Satan bound for the duration of that millennium, sealed in a deep pit and no longer able to deceive humanity. People are liberated from the deceit of the devil, the source of evil in this world as far as the Revelation is concerned, and freed to take innocent pleasure during a thousand years of joy.

Millennialism or "chiliasm," from the word for "thousand" in either Latin (*mille*) or Greek (*khilia*), refers to belief in this epoch of delight. The Revelation's millennium seized the imaginations of the first readers of the book, because those who had been executed unjustly under Roman persecution receive millennial vindication in this vision. "This," says the seer, "is the first resurrection." And he pursues his vision:

> Blessed and holy is he that has a part in the first resurrection; over these the second death has no authority, but they will be priests of God and of Christ, and they will reign with him the thousand years. (Rev 20:5b-6)

This is a collective reign (see also 20:4), and it continues even beyond the thousand years, into the time when Satan will be briefly loosed from his prison, only to be killed along with his minions, who then die the "second"—and permanent—death.

The Revelation climaxes with a seven distinct visionary signs (chapters 17–22) that complete the book's structure of repeated series of seven. The millennium is the central sign in this last and climactic series, the fourth of the seven visionary signs. In the first, the whore of Babylon (the Roman Empire) is destroyed (17:1–19:5), while the second vision celebrates the Wedding of the Lamb (19:6-10). The Lamb here represents Jesus as risen from the dead and alive in heaven, but Jesus also appears in the third sign as the conquering Word of God defeating all enemies (19:11-21). Then comes the millennium (20:1-6), the fourth sign, followed by the final, cosmic war of Gog and Magog (sign five, 20:7-10), divine judgment (sign six, 20:11-15), and the new Jerusalem (sign seven, 21:1–22:6).

The Revelation blends what seem to be predictions concerning time—most obviously, of a thousand years—with visions such as the Wedding of the Lamb that appear to be symbols of eternal and celestial truth rather than events on earth. The millennium is central to the Revelation and to its interpretation, so that we should consider the mixture of statements about it, temporal and celestial, within the text.

Celebration of the millennium, according to the Revelation, does not have to wait for Satan to be bound. Already, in the chapter previous to the reference to the millennium, all who fear God, small and great, praise the Almighty as *already* victorious. The second of the last visions, the Wedding of the Lamb—the celestial animal that is the primary symbol of Jesus throughout the Revelation—calls for festivity (Rev 19:5-10). His bride, the church, is prepared. She wears fine linen, which is identified with the righteous acts of the saints (19:8). "Saints," here and elsewhere in the New Testament, does not refer to individuals of special piety, or to heroes of faith canonized by the church, but to all the people of God, called the "holy ones" (which is what *hagioi* means in the Greek language).

The announcement "Blessed are those invited to the Wedding Supper of the Lamb," in chapter 19, verse 9, is the counterpart of the blessing pronounced in chapter 20, verse 6, on those who have a part in the first resurrection. Because the Revelation is a visionary text, it balances statements in regard to heaven with assertions of what is to occur on the earth.

The Wedding Supper of the Lamb, the second sign, relates to the darker vision of the Word of God pursuing enemies to the point that they are devoured by birds in the third sign (Rev 19:18). This punitive feast is inspired by the book of Ezekiel in a passage that also prophesies the death of Gog, God's enemy on the field of battle (Ezek 39:11, 17-19; see also Rev 20:8, the fifth of the final signs). Once John's visions are read in terms of the biblical precedents upon which they draw, their coherence becomes much clearer. He uses the prophets in the Scriptures of Israel in order to frame a way of seeing human experience in the light of unfolding pictures of events in heaven.

The blessing of those who take part in the feast of the Wedding of the Lamb also echoes the imagery of Jesus' teaching, especially his parable of a wedding feast in Matthew (22:2-14); Luke's version of that parable (14:16-24) finds its preface when a follower of Jesus says, "Blessed is he who will eat bread in the kingdom of God" (14:15). Worship during meals among Jesus' followers was called "the Supper of the Lord," as Paul shows in the earliest written record concerning what later was called the Eucharist (1 Cor 11:20-26). This corresponds with what John of Patmos calls "the Supper of the Lamb" (Rev 19:9), a celestial feast as well as a common meal.

In the ritual setting of the Eucharist, Paul explains that worshippers "announce the Lord's death until he comes" (1 Cor 11:26). The Lord's Supper anticipated the ultimate feast. For John of Patmos, the Wedding Supper of the Lamb combined an awareness that Jesus was the Lamb who was slain *and* the Lamb who received eternal worship in heaven (a theme of the Revelation since 5:11-14).

The relationship between the Wedding Supper of the Lamb and the actual worship of the church explains why this vision is so important for John of Patmos. The Eucharist anticipates the millennium and celebrates its victory. The Revelation's closing vision is of the new Jerusalem that is to descend from heaven (chapter 21). In that city, the "Lord God Almighty is its temple, and the Lamb" (21:22). The Lamb that is Christ takes the place of the temple that the Romans had destroyed in 70 CE, so that the Wedding Supper of the Lamb anticipates the millennial resolution of human history.

The issue of the temple emerged with its destruction by the Romans, a catastrophe for the whole of Judaism that ended the sacrificial practice mandated by the covenant of Moses. Most of those who believed in Jesus prior to 70 CE, whether they were Jewish or not, also saw Jerusalem's temple as the center from which God would act for the world as a whole. In Jesus' words, quoting Isaiah 56:7, the temple was to be "a house of prayer for all nations" (Mark 11:17).

What had become, then, of God's choice of Jerusalem as the place where he would be worshipped one day by all nations? How could sacrifice be offered according to God's will? The

Apocalypse addressed these challenges with the claim that the true place of worship, the real sacrifice that God desired, had been reserved in heaven even as it was being revealed to John of Patmos. For John and those who shared his vision, the temple that the Romans had burned stood for a much deeper reality: the Wedding Supper of the Lamb—when the followers of Jesus were united to him in Eucharist—was the heavenly truth that one day would be realized on earth, as in heaven.

Near the same time the Revelation was written, the Epistle to the Hebrews (ca. 95 CE) also portrayed Christ as the truth underlying sacrificial worship. Hebrews asserted in the wake of the temple's destruction that the temple with its various offerings had existed for all the centuries it did for a single and purely preliminary purpose: to prophesy the perfect sacrifice of Christ. When Christ died, he entered into the heavenly sanctuary, completing every requirement of the law of Moses and showing that only his offering could be fully pleasing to God (Heb 9). The burning of Jerusalem and the ruin of the temple under the Roman general Titus in 70 CE showed that the old covenant really was old (Heb 8:13), merely a foretaste of the new and eternal covenant.

While Hebrews develops a changeless image in heaven, making Christ's sacrifice an eternal reality,[2] in the Revelation the images of Jesus are anything but static. The Lamb that was slain develops sequentially as a Lion (Rev 5:5), a bridegroom at his wedding feast (19:7), and the conquering Word of God (19:13). In the last role, he has power to bind Satan, and ultimately to appear with God in order to constitute the temple in the new Jerusalem (21:22) in a sequence of acts that changes conditions on the earth as the heavenly imagery changes. Both Hebrews and the Apocalypse deal with eternity, but in Hebrews the eternal is changeless, "yesterday and today the same, and forever" (13:8), while in the Revelation it varies, so that both heaven and earth experience change. Revelation's eternity is dynamic, rather than static.

The thousand years of joy, anticipated by John of Patmos, involves a new Jerusalem (Rev 21), the changing imagery of the Lamb that was slain (from Rev 5 onward), and a sequence of final judgment that peaks in the millennium. These visions answer the question of what God will do in response to the temple's destruction. But as we have seen, the Revelation's visions refer both to earth and to heaven, often mixing the two. Is the millennium in chapter 20 a temporal period of a thousand years, or rather a symbol of vindication whose meaning is determined by the celestial Wedding Supper of the Lamb in chapter 19 of the book?

Interpretation of the Revelation has often fixed on the issue of the millennium. During the second century, many Christians saw the Apocalypse as a map to the moment of a total reversal in fortunes, so that they would no longer confront persecution at the hands of the Romans. For them, it was apparent that the millennium was an imminent reward for righteousness.

Papias—Bishop of Hierapolis in Asia Minor[3] during the first half of the second century CE—emerged as a prominent teacher of this point of view. He lead congregations in a city in the same region where the seven letters of the Revelation were sent, and where martyrdom at the hands of the Romans had become a grisly reality. (The execution of one his colleagues in 156 CE, Bishop Polycarp of Smyrna, spurred an entire literature of martyrdom.) Papias taught that believers would not only emerge unscathed from Roman persecution, but also live in millennial delight in a condition akin to Adam and Eve's in paradise. The thousand years were to be a definitive transformation on earth, determined by the visionary signs of John's Apocalypse.

Papias' literary work has been largely lost, except for quotations in the works of later writers. Some of those who quoted Papias ridiculed him, dismissing his teaching as crude materialism. We will consider their criticisms in the next chapter, but they clearly demeaned Papias unfairly. His approach involved a startling but calibrated application of John of Patmos' visions.

Irenaeus, one of Papias' sympathizers from later in the second century, quoted a saying that Papias had attributed to Jesus. It encapsulates how Papias thought this world would be transformed according to the signs of the Apocalypse:

> The days will come in which vines shall grow, each having ten thousand branches, and in each branch ten thousand twigs, and in each true twig ten thousand shoots, and in every one of the

> shoots ten thousand clusters, and in every one of the clusters ten thousand grapes; and every grape when pressed will give two hundred and twenty-five gallons. And when any one of the saints shall lay hold of a cluster, another shall cry out, "I am a better cluster: take me. Bless the Lord through me." In like manner he said that a grain of wheat would produce ten thousand ears, and that every ear would have ten thousand grains, and every grain would yield ten pounds of clear, pure, fine flour; and that apples and seeds and grass would produce in similar proportions; and that all animals, feeding then only on the productions of the earth, would become peaceable and harmonious, and he in perfect subjection to man. (*Against Heresies* 5.33.3)[4]

Papias' image uses the thousand years of Revelation 20:2 as a multiplier to develop each description. Likewise, his introduction of the grapes and winemaking extrapolates the promise of living from the tree of life in Revelation 22:2. The millennium promised by John is Papias' baseline, from which he extrapolated the description of the vineyard.

Papias spoke in the visionary idiom of the Apocalypse and deployed its symbolic arithmetic. In fact, another second-century apocalypse relates the prophecy of the millennial vineyard, with its increasing magnitude of thousands of vats of wine, but instead attributes it all to a heavenly voice, rather than to Jesus. The text involved, called *2 Baruch* or *Apocalypse of Baruch*, influenced both Jewish and Christian belief. (It is classed with the Pseudepigrapha, works widely read by Jews and Christians, but not considered part of the canon.)[5] Papias spoke with the authority of a similarly strong and realistic eschatology that saw no virtue in denying the palpable joys promised by God.

At the same time, the depiction of millennial bliss is by no means simply a matter of ordinary pleasures writ large. Rather, Papias' dedication to a principle of transformation means that, although the joy involved is tangible, it exceeds anything that might be experienced now.

Irenaeus quotes Papias within a work from circa 180 CE devoted to what he calls a *Refutation and Overthrow of Knowledge Falsely So-Called* (and has since been referred to as *Against*

Heresies). Irenaeus' design is to argue against the Gnosticism of his time, which depicted the physical world we live in as hopelessly debased as compared to the spiritual realm of God.[6] One of Irenaeus' principal arguments is that God created the world and will vindicate the righteous in the world. To make that case, he refutes the gnostic conception that another divine power, a lesser divinity, was responsible for the material universe, and also insists that the resurrection promised by God must be in the flesh, rather than purely spiritual.

Just before he cites Papias, Irenaeus goes out of his way to argue that when Jesus promised his followers that they would drink wine new in the kingdom of God, that meant they would also have new flesh (*Against Heresies* 5.33.1; cf. Mark 14:25). Papias' expectation and Irenaeus' use of his teaching set out a coherent reading of the Apocalypse together with a comprehensive theory of human fate.

The Revelation pictures the restored end-time as an epoch of surreal fertility, when the inhabitants of the new Jerusalem will be more than adequately sourced by the fruits of the earth. The risen Jesus in the section of the book that celebrates the Wedding Supper of the Lamb (19:6-10) is also identified as the judge of all, mounted on a white horse, whose name is "the Word of God" (19:11-16). He treads the winepress of God's wrath, imagery taken from Isaiah 63:3 and extended in Julia Ward Howe's "Battle Hymn of the Republic" and John Steinbeck's *The Grapes of Wrath*. These are not bare, literal grapes for John of Patmos, Papias, Howe, or Steinbeck.

Yet grapes remain grapes, even when they signify more than themselves. Once they are trodden they become wine, and the magnificent provision that comes from God and the Lamb is not merely symbolic in Papias' understanding of the Revelation. He was not in the least shy about a material reward for the just. The appeal of the vision of eschatological wine (that is, wine for the *eskhaton*, the final or ultimate state of humanity) resonated for centuries. The Quran—although counseling avoidance of alcohol in this life (Al-Baqara 2.219; Al-Maeda 5.90)—nonetheless vividly describes *rivers* of wine in paradise (Muhammad 47.15; Al-Mutaffifin 83.25).

The new Jerusalem that is the church, portrayed as Christ's own bride at this wedding feast, extends to well over ten thousand square miles in order to accommodate the myriads of people who are to enjoy the wedding feast (Rev 21:16). How are they to be supplied, as well as accommodated? A river of the water of life cascades from the throne of God and the Lamb, while beside it the tree of life produces twelve harvests, one each month. Every part of this tree conveys life: "the leaves of the tree for the healing of the nations" (Rev 22:1-2).

Papias appreciated the primordial sense of this tree. The tree of life had been one of two trees that stood in paradise; it was planted by God along with the tree of the knowledge of good and evil (Gen 2:9). When Adam ate from the tree of knowledge, he was expelled from the garden, for the particular reason that God did not want Adam and his wife to eat from the tree of life, which would have given them an immortality like God's (Gen 3:22).

John of Patmos insisted that the millennium involves bridging the division between God and humanity. In the Revelation, the paradise of Adam and Eve is not only restored, but also completed. Those in the new Jerusalem enjoy a giant, urban garden, where they feast (not merely eat) from the tree of life that was denied to the progeny of Adam and Eve. The millennium and the new Jerusalem it foreshadows are newer and better creations than Eden in "a new heaven and a new earth" (Rev 21:1).

The new Jerusalem had to be enormous to accommodate all those who are to live there eternally—the 144,000 of Israel *and* the myriads and myriads from the Gentiles (according to the vision in Rev 7:4-17). Production from the tree of life reaches a gargantuan scale in John's vision. One harvest per month, in the vision of John, means produce of literally tens of thousands of individual fruits, of every manner of the earth's yield. So when Papias spoke of the wine at the Wedding Feast of the Lamb, he was applying the same scale proposed in the Revelation for the nourishment and healing of Israel and the nations.

Papias no more invented the magnitude of the vineyard than he invented the millennial logic behind it: both are embedded in the Revelation. A thousand years of joy were to bring not merely the restoration of the paradise of Genesis but the enhancement of paradise, so that the power of the tree of life would be available alongside the tree of knowledge, whose fruit has already been with humanity since the fall of Adam. The Apocalypse completes the cosmic story of all creation.

The theme of return to an enhanced paradise presents the history of humanity as an epic in which knowledge and life are realized after a cosmic struggle. Both Papias and John of Patmos shared this theme with other writers of their time. The whole canvas of human history stretched, on this view, from Eden in the primordial past to paradise in the eschatological future. This worldview was parsed by German scholarship more than a century ago, so that the hope embedded in this cyclical perspective became clear:[7] *Urzeit* (the time before time could be reckoned) reflected the *Endzeit* (time after the last moment of history when the meaning of human existence at last came to completion).

This perspective appears in a Jewish pseudepigraphical writing from the same period as the Revelation of John, conventionally known as 4 Ezra—or as 2 Esdras (its title in the Apocrypha of the Christian canon).[8] Both the Revelation of John and 4 Ezra respond to the fact of the destruction of the temple at the hands of the Romans in 70 CE, although they do so in somewhat different ways. Fourth Ezra articulates the explicit promise that "for you Paradise has been opened, the Tree of Life has been planted" (4 Ezra 8:52). Like John of Patmos, "Ezra" believed that the tree of life was to become available to people in the time to come. That appears to have been a part of apocalyptic expectation at the close of the first century CE.

A contrast with the expectation of 4 Ezra comes when the seer of Patmos explicitly states of the new Jerusalem: "I did not see a temple in the city, because the Lord God Almighty is its Temple, and the Lamb" (Rev 21:22). With a single sentence, John changes both the layout of the heavenly city and the usual focus of apocalyptic vision in Judaism. The new Jerusalem includes nothing like an earthly temple, and even the celestial temple—a persistent reference in the Revelation (3:12; 7:15; 11:1, 19; 14:15; 15:5-6, 8; 16:1, 17)—appears as the abode of God rather than as the place where sacrifice is offered. In this, a fundamental expectation of 4 Ezra (and of Daniel in the Hebrew Bible) is altered.

Like 4 Ezra the Revelation combines earthly eschatology (in a messianic reign on earth) with heavenly eschatology (a new age or new world). Yet although the Revelation has made the thousand-year reign of the saints seem conventional in Western thought and literature, it was not so originally. Why should their reign be so long, when it is only a preamble to God's definitive victory over the devil? 4 Ezra speaks of less than half that time, four hundred years, when those with the Messiah will reign with him (7:28).

The Revelation depicts the messianic epoch as "the first resurrection" (20:5), when the Messiah (Christ) rules with his saints. After that millennium come the war of Gog and Magog, the end of Satan and the beast and final judgment (20:7-15), and the new heaven and new earth. They bring with them the new Jerusalem from heaven (21:1-2), where God and the Lamb take the place of the temple (21:22). The saints in the new Jerusalem incorporate that divine presence in the way the sanctuary once did (22:3).

Papias and those who thought as he did believed that the thousand years of joy were extended precisely for the pleasure of the saints, and that they marked the transition to final judgment. That was why a material millennium was no embarrassment to them whatsoever. Along with the vindication of the saints comes the punishment of the wicked, a theme that is worked out side by side with the glories of salvation.

Christ is armed with a sword and a rod of iron (Rev 19:15),[9] in order to defeat and rule the Gentiles, and he treads the winepress of God's wrath. But this image forms only a prelude. An angel calls to all the birds of the air to join in "the great supper of God," a feast on "flesh of kings and flesh of generals and flesh of warriors and flesh of horses and those who sit on them and flesh of all—free and slave and small and great" (Rev 19:18; an image taken from Ezek 39:17-20). A last attempt by the beast and his allies to defeat Christ, a repeated pattern of rebellion throughout the Apocalypse, results only in their consignment to the lake of fire (Rev 19:19-21). This lake endures even beyond the thousand years, to become the ultimate resting place of Satan after his final (20:10, 14–15), disastrous attempt to recruit Gog and Magog in a war against heaven itself (20:7–9; see also Ezek 38:2).

These repeated rebellions underscore the justice of the final judgment, in which not only the enemies of God, but even death and hades are thrown into the lake of fire (Rev 20:14). All that is left is vindication or the abyss in the second and final resurrection.

A thousand years is not too long a preamble for all that to be worked out. The millennium represents a hope not so much for personal vindication as for resolution of the tension between the experience of evil and the promise of divine justice. The basic optimism of this hope is signaled by the conviction that when the deceiver, Satan, is bound (Rev 20:2–3), people will no longer be in thrall to evil.

After the time of Papias, a more comprehensive view of the millennium developed, in which the thousand-year reign of the saints was taken to be the culmination of several millennia. Ancient Stoic teachers had developed the theory of an *ekpurosis*, a fiery conflagration that brings an end to epochs in the rhythm of time.[10] For the Stoics these events were less matters of immediate, divine intervention than the working out of divine principles over many thousands of years. Christian thinkers borrowed Stoic concepts, but foreshortened this expectation.

Stoic thinkers also claimed a form of immortality of the soul, so that human nature enjoyed a natural permanence.[11] The Christian theologian Tertullian, writing circa 208 CE (*De anima* 55.4–5[12]), cited Stoic teaching in order to refute it. He developed an alternative view from his reading of the Revelation: those who inhabited the new Jerusalem during the first resurrection were *exclusively* the martyrs, not humanity as a whole. They alone were under the altar in Revelation 6:9-10, waiting to be released for the period of millennial recompense, and alone merited the first resurrection in Tertullian's opinion. All others would have to await the second resurrection.

Papias' and Tertullian's successors placed their expectation of the final millennium at the close of a series of thousand-year periods, offering a chronologically comprehensive form of apocalyptic expectation. The logic of this development was biblical to some extent. In Genesis God made the world in six days and rested on the seventh day (1:3–2:3)—and to him a day is like a thousand years, and a thousand years as a day (Ps 90:4; 2 Pet 3:8).[13] On this understanding, the millennium promised by John of Patmos would occur six thousand years after the creation; this chronology was spelled out as early as the third century CE.

Once the systematic conception of seven millennia was accepted, the Apocalypse could be mined further in order to locate human experience within that entire calendar. Revelation 17:10 speaks of five "kings" out of seven as already having fallen. If each king represents a thousand years, we are not far from the end. One influential commentator of the third century, Hippolytus of Rome, pressed the line of millennial computation further, assuming the mathematical consistency of the entire Bible in all of its details. The ark of the covenant measured five and a half cubits (2½ by 1½ by 1½), and Hippolytus took that to be a chronological clue. If you translate each cubit into a millennium, that means that after 5,500 years from Adam—that is, 500 years into the reign of the sixth king—Christ would be born (*Commentary on Daniel* 4:23-24).[14] Therefore the interval between Christ's birth and the seventh "week," the millennium promised by John, was exactly 500 years.

Hippolytus' scheme elegantly combined eschatological urgency with philosophical breadth. Yet as the year 500 CE approached, and then receded into memory, his formulation and those like it wore thin.

Millenarian readings of the Revelation have nonetheless proven resilient over time. Papias made the thousand-year reign of the saints into a way of construing human experience as the theater in which, at the end of the day, a just God must endorse and vindicate what is right. The principal challenge to millenarianism came, not from internal faults within the approach or from calendrical disappointments, but from a diametrically opposed approach to understanding everything that the Revelation of John stands for, the topic of the next chapter.

Further Reading

The topic of ancient Christian millenarianism or chiliasm has been a focus of research. Accessible works include John M. Court, *Approaching the Apocalypse: A Short History of Christian Millenarianism* (London: Tauris, 2008); and Stephen Hunt, ed., *Christian Millenarianism from the Early Church to Waco* (Bloomington: Indiana University Press, 2001). For a broader horizon, but focusing on messianic issues, see Magnus Zetterholm, ed., *The Messiah in Early Judaism and Christianity* (Minneapolis: Fortress, 2007). A more technical study is offered by M. C. Steenberg in *Irenaeus on Creation: The Cosmic Christ and the Saga of Redemption*, Supplements to Vigiliae Christianae 91 (Leiden: Brill, 2008). See also Miroslav Marcovich, ed., *Iustini Martyris Dialogus cum Tryphone*, Patristische Texte und Studien (Berlin: de Gruyter, 1997); Philippe Bobichon, *Justin Martyr: Dialogue avec Tryphon, Édition Critique*, Paradosis 47.1-2 (Fribourg: Academic Press, 2003); and Sara Parvis and Paul Foster, eds., *Justin Martyr and His Worlds* (Minneapolis: Fortress, 2007).

2

Transcendent Power

> And I saw another angel flying in midheaven, having an eternal gospel to announce over those dwelling on the earth—even over every nation and tribe and language and people, saying in a great voice, Fear God and give him glory, because the hour of his judgment has come, and worship him who made the heaven and the earth, and sea and springs of water.
>
> Revelation 14:6-7

Papias and his supporters developed a millenarian lens, through which some readers have understood the Revelation ever since. But other thinkers, from the third century on, pursued apocalyptic visions in a completely different direction. Their alternative perspective on how circumstances on earth relate to deeper heavenly realities revolutionized the way the church's dominant thinkers saw the Apocalypse.

The roots of this revolution were ancient. Long before the Revelation of John was written, apocalyptic literature had emerged in Judaism that was less interested in calendars of final judgment than in the journey of a great seer into heaven. Enoch was the classic hero of this literature, but there were others in the Pseudepigrapha; examples come from the period during and after the composition of the Apocalypse and include Christian as well as Jewish texts.[1] Here apocalypses are most important and informative, not because they offered agendas for the end of time, but because they related mystical journeys to the heavenly throne of God, the reality and power behind all creation. This visionary, yet non-millenarian, orientation influenced gnostic literature during the Christian period.

Popular and attractive though it was, millennialism had not supplanted alternative views of how the experience of injustice could be reconciled with divine justice. Gradually, a different logic of reading the Revelation emerged. Instead of following the text horizontally through time, as the course of events that needed to unfold before the saints could reign, teachers such as Origen (185–253) and Augustine (354–430) saw the Revelation along a vertical axis, the line of ascent into heaven. Their approach eclipsed Papias' interpretation for many centuries.

This emphasis on how God was the transcendent power behind all events, discernible by means of reading the Revelation, resulted sometimes in philosophical speculation (Origen's field), but at other times in a vigorous assertion (such as Augustine's) of the political authority that the saints could *already claim* in the affairs of the Roman Empire. The connection with God's throne that the Revelation offered meant that Christians, looking beyond the superficial forces of this world, might *either* seek refuge in a higher realm, *or* insist that God's power should change the world as we know it. The Apocalypse promised transcendent power—philosophical or political, or both.

In their confidence in this new attitude, these thinkers went out of their way to contradict the by-then traditional millenarian approach to the Revelation. Instead of awaiting the hoped-for millennium, the new interpretation insisted that the millennium had *already arrived*, and was manifest within the virtue—and the increasing power—of the church.

This symbolic reading of the millennium proved durable until the modern period. Even alternative interpretations set out a defense of their positions by claiming they made best sense of this dominant approach, grounded in transcendence, rather than in the expectation of the literal thousand-year reign of the saints.

The causes of this shift from a millenarian to a symbolic view of the book of Revelation can be found in an aspect of the Revelation itself—and of apocalyptic literature as a whole—and also in a tectonic shift in the way in which Christians reflected theologically. Neither variable, taken alone, can explain the extraordinary change in early Christian interpretation. Operating together, however, they produced an interpretative transformation that has endured until our epoch.

The disclosure of the divine, the basic meaning of the term "apocalypse," was taken to be a breakthrough that dissolved time itself. Eternity knew no temporal constraint. The divine transcendence by which God became known to people and transformed their lives could not be constrained, on this view, by the requirements of a particular schedule or even a specific order of events. During grim periods of persecution, the transcendent reading gave Christians a purchase on divine reality that offered them freedom from sometimes appalling conditions on the ground. Heaven was theirs, even as "your enemy the devil prowls around like a roaring lion seeking to devour" (1 Pet 5:8). This appeal to transcendence would also, after the conversion of Constantine, result in a justification *for* violence as a means of transforming this world. Before Christianity had any power to exert, however, a new way of conceiving of the world in relation to God had already transformed its sensibilities.

Platonism and Its Gnostic Succession

As Christianity grew in the Mediterranean world, it adapted to its Hellenistic environment across the fields of language, culture, worldview, and thought. Jesus' movement emerged within the political world of Roman Hellenism and its rule of what Rome eventually called *Syria Palaestinia*. Jesus and his first followers developed their purposes, activities, and message within the microclimate of Aramaic-speaking, Galilean Judaism. The surprising appeal of Jesus and his message within the broader Hellenistic setting outside of Galilee—in predominantly Greek-speaking, Gentile cities rather than in the Aramaic, Judaic countryside that had produced Jesus himself—permitted Christianity to develop and thrive as a religion.

This move into Hellenism brought profound changes, involving thought and feeling, as well as language. Greek-speaking Christians deployed their native worldview as their natural means for understanding their faith from the outset. The emphasis of Christianity shifted as it Hellenized. Jesus had preached "the kingdom of God" as his central message, a principle of the transformation of this world in order to follow the will of God; the phrase carried political overtones, and its challenge to supplant human rule with God's sounded like sedition to many Romans. That is why the kingdom is deemphasized by Hellenistic writers such as Paul. Instead, their central concern is Christ himself, as the ideal of a human being imbued by God's Spirit. The Son of God was the fulcrum of Hellenistic Christianity, while Jesus' emphasis had been on the kingdom of God in his native environment of Aramaic Judaism.

Hellenistic Christians believed that—whether they were Jews or Gentiles, male or female, slave or free—they became a new creation in which God made his Spirit available through Christ to enlighten, guide, and strengthen their identity as God's children (see Gal 3:28; 4:6; 6:15). To them, this was the meaning of baptism, the sacramental gateway to eternal life. In order to convey the full impact of this breakthrough of Spirit, many Christians resorted to the language and concepts of Platonism.

Platonist Christians saw this world as a pale imitation of the substantial reality that endures in heaven alone. The church father Origen, born in 185 CE in Egypt, championed the symbolic reading of the Revelation of John by means of his Platonist understanding of the Scripture. Origen believed that the heavenly world could be known through the Spirit of God, because the Spirit is also the basis of every reality that can be perceived (*On First Principles* 2.3.6). His commitment to the view that heaven completely surpasses the world as we know it put him in overt opposition to the kind of millenarianism that Papias championed, and that other second-century writers (such as Justin and Irenaeus) also espoused.

Origen rejected the whole idea that flesh is involved in the resurrection, even when biblical promises appear to depict earthly joys. He insisted that people who see resurrection that way "reject the labor of thinking and seek after the outward and literal meaning of the law, or rather give way to their own desires and lusts" (*On First Principles* 2.11.2). With these words Origen ridicules anything like Papias' approach.

Origen dismisses pragmatic millenarianism for both scriptural and theological reasons. Paul is the ground of the apostolic authority Origen invokes, especially the apostle's teaching that in the resurrection a person becomes a "spiritual body," rather than a resuscitated physical body (1 Cor 15:35-55). Origen uses that perspective to assess the Scriptures as a whole according to their spiritual rather than physical meaning (*On First Principles* 2.11.3). But he also deepens his argument from interpretation with a theological appeal. He maintains that the most urgent longing of human beings is the desire to join themselves to God. This longing is as basic to our minds as seeing is to the eye: constitutionally, we long for the vision of God (*On First Principles* 2.11.4).

Although symbolic and often allegorical, the manner in which Origen develops his own thought remains eschatological, but in its own key. In his teaching, after death human souls receive education in paradise prior to entry into the realm of heaven proper; they gradually accommodate to divine reality (*On First Principles* 2.11.6). In this Platonic construction of the Christian faith, eschatology—the teaching of humanity's ultimate end—is at the service of transcendence.

For this reason, Origen's interpretation of the Apocalypse sets its face against any materialism. The heavenly Jerusalem of Revelation 21 refers, not to a city of literal stones, but to "the whole body of Christ constituted by the saints" (*Commentary on John* 10.35.230). Likewise, when the Word of God in Revelation 19:12 is described as having eyes "like a flame of fire," even this is an analogy, referring to Christ's capacity to consume away thoughts that are too material (*Commentary on John* 2.7.57).

In the Revelation, the coming of Christ as the Word of God signals the last judgment. Called "King of kings and Lord of lords" (Rev 19:16), he defeats the beast and his minions, opening the way for the binding of Satan, the millennium, and then the final destruction of evil. The new Jerusalem follows. This is the hope of Christ's "second coming" in judgment, as it is called in English. But the corresponding term in Greek, *parousia*, basically means "presence" rather than "second coming." For Origen this is not in the least a material arrival, but the union of Christ with the believer to such an extent that the believer leaves mortality behind to become one spirit with the Lord. Insofar as movement is involved, it is the believer's toward heaven, rather than Christ's toward earth.

Once Christ's ultimate advent is understood along the lines of Origen's perspective, the meaning of texts in the Revelation as well as in the Gospels appears entirely different from what Papias taught. Origen deliberately dissolved both literal views of Christ's second coming from heaven to earth as well as linear views of time that define and fix the end of history within a calendar. He conceived of hell as a disintegration of the soul, rather than a permanent place of torment; the fire of judgment may even have a remedial effect in his view because God can use it to purify a soul (*On First Principles* 2.10.5). Since the completion of creation (its *apokatastasis*) continued beyond this world into the realm of the resurrection, Origen also held that even Satan, if he repented, could be forgiven (*Against Celsus* 4.65). Origen routinely dismissed the expectation of a literal reign of Christ with the saints lasting precisely one thousand years, and his attacks on millenarianism conceived of in that way are explicit and repeated.

The only time that truly matters in Origen's approach is the interval until one's personal death, which determines experience in paradise and in the resurrection. "Heaven," as a place beyond this world, now occupies the central position once occupied by the eschatological kingdom of God in Jesus' teaching. Platonism had transformed the meaning of Christianity. Origen's genius was to see the possibility of this transformation, and to work out its implications. Some of his signature concepts bear the clear imprint of Gnosticism, which also converted the genre of apocalypse into a uniquely vertical dimension. Much of Gnosticism's literature claimed to be a "revelation" or "apocalypse" to teachers such as Paul, Peter, and John.[2] Like some gnostic thinkers Origen took up the possibility that God could create parallel worlds. If the providential task of bringing all creatures to their completion was not brought to term in this world, God could create another, and another, and another. Because Origen imagined that God could create another world and arrange for beings to transmigrate to the new creation, he has been said to teach a version of reincarnation, but the idea of repeated, individual lives was far from Origen's mind. His point was rather that physical duration on the earth could not limit the power and wisdom of God (*On First Principles* 1.7.5, 3.5.4). After all, time is no constraint on God; limitation to time is one of the great faults of literal millenarianism both for Origen and for the gnostics.

Later councils of the church condemned what they called "Origenism," the allegedly heretical aspect of Origen's theology. His thought experiment in regard to Satan's repentance brought his reputation no end of trouble. As we will see later in this chapter, Christian Platonists after Origen saw Satan, evil, sin, and their consequences as *permanent* realities that not even God would change. The very idea of Satan's repentance seemed an oxymoron from this later point of view.

Origen's approach to eschatology, on the other hand, proved triumphant. He recalibrated the axis of reading the Revelation and similar texts from the horizontal concern of history to the vertical aspiration of transcendence. Despite his posthumous condemnation, Origen's approach persisted. There is evidence that he preached and wrote on the Revelation, although his detailed work on the text is now lost.[3] Yet the fundamental perspective of his approach to the text becomes plain, when Origen refers to the angel preaching the everlasting gospel in Revelation 14:10 as signifying a heavenly comprehension of the truth that surpasses present understanding—as much as the new covenant supersedes the old. This signature conception, whose key text appears at the outset of this chapter, marked a new understanding of the Revelation as a whole.

By approaching the Revelation in this way, Origen assured that his followers would see the text as a transcendent message, rather than as a linear, eschatological scenario that needed time in order to be fulfilled. For Origen, even the sun and moon, although splendid to human eyes, are fallen entities imprisoned in physical bodies in order to maintain the *illusion* of time (*First Principles* 2.8.7, 3.6.8, 4.2.4, 4.3.12-13). He taught fellow Christians to see time as a misapprehension from the perspective of eternity, and to appreciate the eternal gospel of the Revelation as a gift to humanity—insight into the everlasting structure of heaven. For all the vicissitudes his reputation suffered at the hands of orthodoxy after his death, Origen succeeded in providing catholic, orthodox Christianity with a vision of the Revelation that offered a powerful alternative to millenarianism and that lasted longer than any other single interpretation.

Worship and Apocalypse

The influence of Origen's interpretation was extended by his student, Dionysius of Alexandria, who became the bishop of that city. Dionysius developed an early critical view of the authorship of the Apocalypse; on stylistic grounds he correctly denied that the same person wrote the Fourth Gospel and the Revelation. Like Origen before him, he insisted that the Revelation could not be understood as a prediction of earthly events, so that the millennium should not be taken literally. In fact, he even maintained that it is *impossible* to understand the text in literal terms. To Dionysius' mind, this did not make the Revelation nonsensical. Rather, problems of understanding in terms of prediction only established the text's idiom as one of mystery: "For if I do not understand I suspect that a deeper sense lies beneath the words" (see Eusebius, *History of the Church* 3.25.4-6, our source for Dionysius' remarks). The conviction that the Revelation signals a deeper sense strengthened the appeal of symbolic interpretation.

Dionysius' sense of the meaning of the book, as pointing to realities beyond words, lies behind the most pervasive usage of the Revelation within the Christian tradition in every epoch: worship, as a means of approaching God for purposes of prayer, celebration, and lament. Unlike the Psalms—another key scriptural component of worship—the consistent point of view of the Revelation is not that of human beings seeking God. Instead, the Revelation invites worshippers to take the perspective of heaven, and look at conditions on earth from that transcendent point of view.

No book in the New Testament exceeds the Revelation of John in the proportion of material devoted to worship. The force of this emphasis is all the stronger, because the worship concerned is not in the form of liturgical instructions to communities, but involves descriptions of how God is adored within the heavenly court of angels, spirits, and powers.

Passages from the Revelation have echoed in Christian liturgies for two millennia. The praise of God on his heavenly throne in Revelation 4:8 is perhaps the best example: "Holy, holy, holy, Lord God Almighty, who was and is and is to come." The wording—the term "holy" used three times—takes up the hymn of the seraphim in Isaiah 6:3. But in the Apocalypse, the hymn is extended to refer to God's rule over all time and space.

The location of this hymn within the Revelation helps to explain its influence. After his letters to the seven churches, John of Patmos describes a gate opened into heaven, which permits him to go up and to see the throne of God (4:1–5:14). The divine throne was a master symbol within Near Eastern religion, in evidence from the third millennium BCE across several civilizations: the center of divine power, creativity, judgment, and compassion. Contact with rituals of divine power also influenced Roman civic devotion to the rule of the gods and of emperors;[4] the Apocalypse sees divinity without the mediation of any human empire, as disclosure to faithful believers.

In the Revelation's depiction of the seer's heavenly ascent, the throne is set behind seven lamps of fire, identified as the seven spirits of God, and a crystal sea. The last image is a precise link to worship, because the "crystal sea" (Rev 4:6) corresponds to the basin in the sanctuary of the temple, near the altar, which is so large it is described as a "sea" (1 Kgs 7:23-26). Within the temple, the basin represented the primordial waters of creation, just as the holy of holies represented the footstool of God's throne on earth. Notably, the sea in the temple was supported by twelve oxen, a basic number in the Revelation, as well, which is doubled in the description of the throne as surrounded by twenty-four elders.

Sounds and thunder roar from this throne (Rev 4:1-8). Within this setting, special privilege is given to the song of four living creatures, all singing a song of praise to God as creator. Irenaeus in the second century identified these four creatures—the first like a lion, the second like an ox, the third like a man, and the fourth like an eagle—with the Evangelists (*Refutation* 3.11.8), and this symbolism was taken up by Augustine and Jerome and passed into traditional iconography. Once the Evangelists are so identified, the reading of their gospels is tied to the recitation of the heavenly hymn, which is then presented as the fundamental meaning of their writings.

The celebration of God as "almighty" or "all-ruling" (*pantokrator*) and thrice holy became standard themes in Christian worship, especially in connection with the orthodox Eucharist, where the hymn called *trisagion* ("three times holy") typically featured in the opening of the Divine Liturgy. In the Revelation, the worship of Jesus as the Lamb of God invites recognizing *him* as *pantokrator*, almighty in the same way as God upon his throne.[5] Christ alone is held worthy to break open the seven seals of a scroll on the throne. He is not only the Lamb that appears to have been slain—yet with seven horns and seven eyes that correspond to the seven spirits of God, but also the Lion of the tribe of Judah and the Root of David (Rev 5:5-6). The living creatures and the elders sing to the Lamb, as earlier God the *pantokrator* had been praised: "You are worthy to receive the scroll and to open its seals, because you were slain and purchased for God, by your blood, those from every tribe and tongue and people and nation, and made them a kingdom and priests to our God, and they shall reign upon the earth" (Rev 5:9).

This veneration of the Lamb—who is manifestly more than a lamb, and whose attributes shift as John's experience unfolds—implicitly offers Jesus worship in a manner commensurate with the worship of God. John's vision of the throne, as set out in chapters 4 and 5, is the pivot of his whole book. So powerful is this material that the Revelation's identification of *Christ* as *pantokrator* became a prominent theme within orthodoxy, and icons that specifically identify him in this way have commonly been found in Orthodox churches throughout the centuries. This amounts to the visual approval of the transcendent and christological interpretation of the Revelation, as against a millenarian reading.

John of Patmos sees the throne, the divine source of creation, in language associated with Moses, who in Exodus 24:10 saw God enthroned, and the prophet Ezekiel, who depicted the details of the chariot throne in the first chapter of his book. Steeped as this vision is in the biblical imagery of the divine throne, it also incorporates the distinctively Christian experience of Jesus' resurrection. He appears with the one on the throne, as the Lamb that was slain (Rev 5:12-13). But his slaying led to his resurrection (1:18) and exaltation, and joins him to the throne of God. The Lamb's triumph elicits a hymn of praise (5:9-10) because the one who was slain acquires saints from every people to reign on earth forever.

The vision of God and the Lamb in chapters 4 and 5 stands at the juncture of the seer's movement from earth to heaven, because he sees a door opening into higher realities in Revelation 4:1, just before the vision begins. This opens the way to continuing refinement of the image in the experience of worship;[6] within the Revelation the Lamb might appear as slain, or as triumphant, or as a Lion. Those are not contradictions, but patterns that provide worshippers with means to relate their conditions to the reality of heaven. Because the Revelation depicts a heavenly reality, its elements were natural components of worship in communities that believed they joined the heavenly choirs when they were at prayer.

Worshippers sang what John of Patmos heard the angels say, and repeated words that also echoed the praise of the thrice-holy God sung by the seraphim reported by Isaiah (6:1-3). Just as the divine chorus looked to a divine reality that was and is and is to come (Rev 1:4, 8; 4:8), so their words were drawn from prophecy in the concern for past, present, and future. Prophets, whether in the Hebrew Bible or the New Testament, did not articulate basic foundations of worship because they aspired to be liturgists. Rather, the power of their visions was incorporated within the heavenly universe that communities called their adherents to esteem higher than any power on earth.

Calling God *pantokrator* means he is "almighty" in the precise sense that he *rules* (*krateo* in Greek) all things as well as creates them. When orthodoxy, following the association of the Lamb with the throne in the Revelation, worships Jesus as the *pantokrator*, that is a strong claim that the whole of experience is ultimately under Christ's control.

The Power of Transcendence

Constantine's toleration of Christianity, the dramatic end of persecution, and the emperor's eventual embrace of the once-despised faith caused thinkers within the church such as Eusebius (260–340 CE) to conclude that an epochal change in all history had swept aside old ways. In Eusebius' view the new regime introduced the golden age of the church as well as of the empire. The victory of Constantine and his colleague Licinius (who at first reigned with Constantine) was nothing less than the appointed plan of God within a definite intervention within human events.

Eusebius reminds his readers of the terrible tortures Christians had experienced, and then proceeds to describe the difference that Constantine made:

> But once again the Angel of the great counsel, God's great Commander-in-Chief, after the thoroughgoing training of which the greatest soldiers in his kingdom gave proof by their patience and endurance in all trials, appeared suddenly and thereby swept all that was hostile and inimical into oblivion and nothingness, so that its very existence was forgotten. But all that was near and dear to him he advanced beyond glory in the sight of all, not men only but the heavenly powers as well—sun, moon, and stars, and the entire heaven and earth. (*History of the Church* 10.4.15)

Only the language of apocalypse, the sequenced revelation of God himself in Christ, can explain to Eusebius' satisfaction how the former agony can so quickly have been transformed into festivity. The promised future had begun under Constantine, and there was no room for a return to the past.

In his *History of the Church*, Eusebius presents a theologically structured political history according to which Constantine restored the united form of the empire that had been the ideal of

Augustus, the first emperor (10.9.6-9). Carefully placing Christ's birth during Augustus' reign, after the Roman subjugation of Egypt (1.5), Eusebius then pairs Christ and Constantine as the realization of the imperial ideal. That opened the way for a new reading of the Revelation. The millennium no longer marked the end of human experience; instead, history unfolds *in* the millennium for Eusebius. Historical patterns showed that the church now lived during the reign of the saints—politically, not only as a matter of prayerful vision. The daring of Eusebius' move has exerted an impact ever since his time.

Eusebius directly contradicted the millenarianism of Papias and his followers. Eusebius dismissed Papias as a man of small intelligence, saying so without mincing words (*History of the Church* 3.39.1-17). Unfortunately for Papias' reputation, Eusebius is a major source of Papias' teaching. In particular, Eusebius made fun of Papias' description of the material joys that the millennium was to include.

The myriads of wine barrels and stores of fine food that entranced Papias had no appeal for Eusebius. As far as Eusebius was concerned, such expectations were simplistic distortions, because the true meaning of the Revelation could only be interpreted "mystically," according to its true intention (*History of the Church* 3.39.12). Eusebius rejected the idea that the thousand years offered literal pleasures, denying that chronological time was not involved at all (7.25.1-5). In the Christian Platonist tradition he saw the Revelation's millennium as symbolic.

Yet Eusebius did not reject the Revelation of John, whether as part of the canon or in the substance of its vision. He was only anti-millenarian in his blunt opposition to Papias, and dealt with the Revelation's millennium itself by means of interpretation rather than denial. To his mind, the thousand years are an epoch when Satan no longer enslaves humanity. When Eusebius looked to the recent past, during the period when the power of the Roman Empire persecuted those who believed in Christ, he saw the image of the beast from the sea that vaunted itself and blasphemed (Rev 13:1-9), as fulfilled by the third-century Emperor Valerian (*History of the Church* 7.10.2), who had been defeated and captured at Edessa by the Persian ruler, Shapur I. By

Eusebius' time, Christians saw Valerian's fate as an example of the ignominious punishment of persecutors of the church.[7]

Eusebius believed that the great turning of the ages had taken place. He pioneered the program to historicize prophecy, so that the distress of the period of Roman persecution was part of an apocalypse; history had already run through the birth pangs that presaged the age of salvation. For Eusebius, however, history was not just a horizontal line of events, but represented the powerful incursion of transcendence into human affairs.

Eusebius was convinced that Christ was at work in Constantine's conversion: "From that time on a day bright and radiant, with no cloud overshadowing it, shone down with shafts of heavenly light on the churches of Christ throughout the world" (*History of the Church* 10.1.8). Everyone enjoyed the benefits involved, because "to all men there was freedom from the oppression of the tyrants" (10.2.1): just as John of Patmos said of the millennium, it was a time when Satan was bound (Rev 20:2-3), so that people were free of his deceit for the first time ever.

Eusebius also believed that the prophetic forecast of a resurrection at this time had been fulfilled in a "mystical" sense, because the gathering of the church under Constantine put together "bone to bone and joint to joint" (10.3.1). This realized the prophecy of Ezekiel (chapter 37), and in the millennium there would be resurrection for those who "had not worshiped the beast or its image and had not received its mark" (Rev 20:4). With the rise of the power of the church under Constantine, mystical resurrection had been realized in Eusebius' understanding. Now was the marriage of the Lamb to his bride, the church, and now the new Jerusalem grew in every place that churches were founded with imperial warrant (*History of the Church* 10.4.2-4).

Eusebius believed that the settlement under Constantine fulfilled prophecy, and he fully articulated this political theology in his *Praise of Constantine.* After speaking of Christ, the Word of God, who holds dominion as an iron scepter over the whole world (following Rev 19:11-16), Eusebius goes on to make a comparison with Constantine: "Our Emperor, beloved of God, bearing a kind of image of the supreme rule as it were in imitation of the greater, directs the course of all things upon earth" (*Praise of Constantine* 1.6). Here the pagan Stoic idea of the rule of the emperor as commensurate with the divine rule is provided with a new substance: the emperor who obeys Christ himself imitates Christ's glory. Jesus, identified in the tradition of John of Patmos as the *pantokrator* in heaven, corresponds to the almighty and pious emperor on the earth.

Christ as *pantokrator,* paired with images of the emperor, became standard in the official iconography. Eusebius believed that he lived in the age of millennial fulfillment. History had not ended, but it had been definitively redeemed. The power of the state, rightly deployed, conveyed the transcendent power of God. This was the axiom of the Roman Empire from the fourth century onward as it established its new capital, Constantinople, on the site of ancient Byzantium. This political theology of Byzantine Christianity dominated there until 1453, when the Ottoman ruler Mehmed II captured the city, and it remains the ideal in much of Orthodox Christianity.

Although Eusebius mounted a severe attack on millennialism and indicated how he preferred to interpret the Revelation of John, the actual program of the new interpretation was worked out by Tyconius in North Africa (whose death is usually placed ca. 390 CE). His work has been left over in incomplete form; he was not a partisan of the Catholic Church that Constantine and his successors authorized. Tyconius was rather a Donatist, one of those who believed that any clergy who had collaborated with the authorities during the persecution of the Romans vitiated their own standing, and that of their successors. Nonetheless, he found a way to explain how John's millennium had already dawned, and influenced Catholic theology after him.

For Tyconius, Scripture as a whole, and the Revelation of John in particular, should not be applied literally. He believed the thousand years of Revelation 20:4 referred to the time between the ascension of Jesus and his *parousia.*[8] During this time, baptism made believers victorious over the deceit of Satan; the number of years was of spiritual rather than literal significance. Prediction was not the purpose of scriptural interpretation.

The setbacks that the newly Christian Empire suffered caused interpreters to see the millennium along the lines Tyconius laid down. Augustine's *City of God*, a work of twenty-three books, responds to the perceived decay of the Empire, signaled to many observers by the sack of Rome at the hands of Alaric in 410 CE. From the outset, Augustine 154sounds his theme, that the city of God is an eternal city that exists in the midst of the city of men; those two cities are both mixed and at odds in this world, but they are to be separated by the final judgment after the millennium (*City of God* 1.1).

History for Augustine is the interplay of these two forces, which determine the existence of every society and every person. In the millennium that comes with the church, love of self is no longer imposed by Satan's deception. Human will is free to be itself, and to create itself in God's image, or fail to do so. Although once a millenarian in the tradition of Papias, Augustine now held that the first resurrection was not literal, but a rebirth of the soul (*City of God* 20.6.2), and that the thousand years were symbolic.

Augustine died in Hippo while the city was under siege by the people called the Vandals. Yet his conception that his history and every history reflected the struggle between the two cities prepared him and the global church for that disaster, and many subsequent disasters. He drew upon the Eusebian model of history as apocalypse, taking it even more seriously than Eusebius himself had. Rather than promise an easy transition to the reign of Christ, and to the moment when God would be all in all, Augustine portrays an apocalyptic history filled with struggle. If history is apocalyptic, then human flesh has indeed been blessed by its transcendent millennium, but living free of Satan's deceit does not rid humanity of a constitutional flaw.

The struggle, however, is not ultimately between good and evil, but between the love of God and the love of self. That is the key to Augustine's ceaseless, pastoral ministry, as well as to his remarkably broad intellectual horizon. In every time and in every place, there is the possibility that the city of God will be revealed and embraced; now, in the millennium he called *Christiana tempora*, we at last know its name.

Augustine's Platonism enabled him to insist that the thousand years of Revelation 20 are not to be taken literally. But if the millennium has indeed come in the present, *Christiana tempora*, then the prophecies *of that same chapter* must involve stringent requirements of real action. His view of history was, at the end of the day, as apocalyptic as the Christian history that Eusebius had designed, crafted to show how heaven would complete events on earth by means of a new transcendent power released within human politics.

The newly converted Roman Empire was to be the instrument of a permanent Christian regime of unlimited power, until Jesus would return to judge the earth. Augustine sanctioned the use of force and violence in this world to deal with heresy. He was known to remark that it was better for the heretics to perish in physical flames than in those of hell (*Epistle* 204.2). Jews and heretics find themselves classed together when Augustine comes to interpret Revelation 20:7-8:

> For this is to be the last persecution, when the last judgment will be at hand, a persecution which will be visited throughout the whole earth upon the holy church, that comprehensive City of Christ, at the hands of the comprehensive city of the devil, each in the full greatness that it shall have on the earth. For those nations, called Gog and Magog, are not to be understood as some barbarian peoples dwelling in some part of the earth. . . . Now we understand that these names mean: Gog, "roof"; Magog, "from the roof"; or, as it were, the house and he who goes forth from the house. (*City of God* 20.11)

"Gog" (from *gag* in Hebrew) is taken to be the house of Israel, Jews who refuse to accept Christ despite all the prophetic prompting and existential evidence that they should, just as "Magog" is taken to be the heretics (see 1 John 2:19 by way of precedent). As Augustine says in *Sermon* 62, "Heretics, Jews and pagans—they have come to form a unity over against our Unity."

Augustine denies the literal millennium, and to that extent shows the influence of Origen, but he does so in a way that nonetheless endorses the view of history as a battlefield of the forces of light against those of darkness. The grounding theme of the two cities meant that Gog and Magog must refer to the perennial opponents of the church that, during her millenarian reign, she must resist, since Satan no longer deceives her. Christian Platonism in Augustine is in a new key as compared to Origen. The issue is not only the human ascent to the realm of transcendence, but also how power reaches down from the transcendent to transform this world.

Even defeated, Satan remained the enemy, and the church was at perpetual war against evil, even during the current, millennial epoch. This aspect of Augustine's thought, a possible influence of his time as a Manichaean prior to his baptism, was embraced by the church. Satan was a necessary enemy, to eternity and beyond. Considering the possibility of Satan repenting and being forgiven was no longer acceptable. The ideal of a church that embodied the millennium instead of awaiting it required permanent evil, in order to demonstrate her independence from Satan's thrall. The church was permanent in this conception, but so was the evil she confronted. The battle between good and evil had not been won, but internalized in the soul of every person. With that dualistic standoff, the Middle Ages began[9] in the conviction that good and evil were evenly matched. In the tension of that perennial struggle, a new approach to the Revelation of John took shape.

Further Reading

Resources for Origen's and Augustine's thought include Ilaria R. E. Ramelli, "Origen's Interpretation of Violence in the Apocalypse," in *Ancient Christian Interpretations of "Violent Texts" in the Apocalypse*, ed. Joseph Verheyden, Tobias Nicklas, and Andreas Merkt (Göttingen: Vandenhoeck & Ruprecht, 2011), 46–62; and Peter Brown, *Augustine of Hippo: A Biography* (Berkeley: University of California Press, 2000).

The late Alan F. Segal dealt with the theme of the journey to the throne in a now classic article, "Heavenly Ascent in Hellenistic Judaism, Early Christianity and Their Environment," *Aufstieg und Niedergang der Romischen Welt,* vol. 2, *Principat* 23, ed. Wolfgang Haase (Berlin: de Gruyter, 1980), 1333–94. The development of commentary on the Revelation that reflects this theme is detailed in Thomas Johann Bauer, *Das tausendjährige Messiasreich der Johannesoffenbarung: Ein literarkiritsche Studie zu Offb 19.11–21.8*, Beihefte zur Zeitschrift für die neutestamentliche Wissenschaft und die Kunde der älteren Kirche 148 (Berlin: de Gruyter, 2007); and illustrated in Nancy Grubb, *Revelations: Art of the Apocalypse* (New York: Abbeville Press, 1997).

For works of Origen cited here, see G. W. Butterworth, *On First Principles: Being Koetschau's Text of the* De Principiis (New York: Harper & Row, 1966); Cécile Blanc, *Origène: Commentaire sur saint Jean*, Sources Chrétiennes 120, 157, 222, 290, 385 (Paris: Editions du Cerf, 1966–1992); and Henry Chadwick, ed. and trans., *Origen: Contra Celsum* (Cambridge: Cambridge University Press, 1980).

3

Oracle of Redemption

> And another sign appeared in heaven, and look: a great red dragon having seven heads and ten horns and upon his heads seven crowns, and his tail swept the third of the stars of heaven and threw them to the earth. And the dragon stood before the woman who was about to give birth, so when she gave birth he could devour her child.
>
> Revelation 12:3-4

Recourse to the Revelation of John as an oracle, capable of guiding people great and small into a dangerous future, became current during the Middle Ages. The rise of this approach can be traced through one of the most famous commentators on the Revelation who ever lived, Joachim of Fiore. He brought together the influences of his time and crafted them into a new way of reading John's text, the Bible, and the meaning of humanity's confrontation with the future. His views exemplify the distinctive type of interpretation of the Apocalypse that had emerged during his time.

Joachim (1135–1202) lived during a period of vision, at a time when Hildegard of Bingen (1098–1179) portrayed "the woman clothed with the sun" in Revelation 12, not merely as the church (the traditional interpretation), but also as Eve and the Virgin Mary.[1] Where Hildegard conveyed her visionary message by illustrations, as well as written works and music, Joachim's approach was analytic.

On pilgrimage to the Kingdom of Jerusalem (as the crusaders called their conquest) around 1167, Joachim traveled to Mount Tabor. Tradition claimed that Jesus had appeared there transfigured to three of his disciples, and spoke with Moses and Elijah (see Mark 9:1-8). There Joachim also claimed that he had a revelation.

Joachim saw a deep concordance running between events in the Old Testament and events in the New Testament, and conceived of the relationship between the Testaments as the twofold law of the Bible. Understanding that correspondence was to his mind the key to understanding the present. His pilgrimage led to his decision to live as a monk in his native Calabria (at the toe of Italy's boot), which at that time the Norman Kingdom of Sicily controlled. He refused to pursue the career in the royal court of Sicily for which his family had prepared him. Joachim followed his own way as a lay preacher and a hermit, but eventually accepted ordination as a priest, association with the monks at Corazzo, and the position of abbot in the monastery.

Joachim and his monastic colleagues were deeply attached to the discipline of poverty. Their means were so scarce that they were denied their wish to be associated with the Cistercian Order, which required the assurance that a monastic house command adequate resources to survive. Although Joachim complained about administrative work, he showed skill in that arena; he managed to secure enough gifts of land and papal preferences so that the Cistercians finally did accept the abbey of Corazzo as their own.

By that time (1188), however, Joachim had papal permission and support to withdraw from Corazzo to a mountain house, San Giovanni in Fiore, where he committed himself and a small staff to a hermetic discipline of writing. He devoted himself above all to the principal project of his adult life: understanding the Revelation of John and its application to history and experience.

Joachim was able to pursue his unusual monastic discipline, which was stringent and at the same time cosseted, because he had earlier impressed Pope Lucius III at a critical point in Joachim's life as well as in the experience of Western Christendom. Any help in divining the events that were shaping the world in often unexpected ways could be of critical use to the papacy. During his negotiation concerning the monastic house at Corazzo in 1184, he took advantage of this interview with Lucius to tell the pope that he understood on the basis of his reading of the Revelation of John that Jerusalem was about to fall to the Saracens (as Christians then typically called Muslims). When Saladin took the city back for Islam three years later, Joachim became famous. Securing Lucius' permission to pursue his literary work, as a commentator on the Revelation and on the meaning of Scripture as a whole, posed Joachim no particular problem.

His reputation for oracular insight into the Revelation—a gift that permitted current events to find their sense in Scripture—made Joachim a likely consultant for the archetypical crusader, Richard I (the Lionhearted). Richard met up with his flotilla in Sicily to proceed on his crusade to take Jerusalem back, and this flamboyant but insecure man of action wanted to know whether he would succeed. The monk had precise advice for the king according to the report of Roger de Hoveden, Richard's chronicler and a witness of the meeting.[2]

Joachim believed by then (early in 1191) that he had solved one of the great enigmas of the Revelation: the identity of the "great red dragon having seven heads" (Rev 12:2). As commentators had done long before his time, Joachim read this vision in terms of the history of the persecution of the church, which was symbolized by the woman clothed with the sun who was about to give birth, whom the dragon threatened (Rev 12:1-4). Joachim's approach made the surreal animal images of the Revelation coincide with the book of Daniel, where beasts arising from the sea stand for persecuting empires (Dan 7).

To Joachim's mind—or as he said, to his mind's eye—the dragon in Revelation 12 corresponds to the beast with seven heads spoken of in Revelation 17:7-11. This principle of correspondence from one part of the book to another was basic to his approach, because Joachim believed that the Apocalypse was structured as a series of recapitulations. The text returned to consider enduring realities and was not constructed as a straight line of time. Five of the dragon's heads had made their appearance, and two were still to come, just as John of Patmos said in Revelation 17:10. But Joachim read this statement in terms of his own time, not the first century, and he identified each head on that basis.

The first head was Herod the Great, who (according to Matthew 2) killed the infants of Bethlehem at the time of Jesus' birth. The second was the Emperor Nero, who ordered Christians tortured and killed, including Peter and Paul. The third was a Roman emperor of the Christian period, Constantius II; he accepted baptism in 361 from a bishop considered a heretic, an Arian who did not believe in Jesus' full divinity. Constantius also named the anti-Christian Julian the Apostate as his successor, which confirmed his inveterate heresy. The fourth was Cosdroe, the king of Persia who had stolen a piece of the true cross and, in Joachim's judgment, prepared the way for Muhammad. The fifth was Mesomothus, a North African dynasty that ruled in Spain during Joachim's time, which Joachim presented as a person.

These figures scarcely stand as historically pivotal from today's vantage point. Some of them have provoked controversy in regard to what precisely Joachim meant to say. When it came to the sixth head, however, Joachim was unambiguous that Saladin was of concern. Finally, the seventh and climactic head was the antichrist, who brought history to its climax.

Even before the time of Joachim, the beast in the Revelation had been associated with the antichrist, although that word does not appear anywhere in the text. The term does appear in other literature named after a "John" (1 John 2:22, 4:3; 2 John 1:7), but in the sense of those who deny Christ, not as Christ's supernatural opponent. For this reason, the plural appears occasionally (e.g., 1 John 2:18). As early as the third century, however, Hippolytus confidently stated that the beast in Revelation 13 is none other than the antichrist (*De Christo et Antichristo* 49[3]). From that time the Apocalypse provided content, by means of its images and wording, to speak of the antichrist in an eschatological sense. Joachim therefore built upon a centuries-old understanding of what the Revelation of John truly meant.

Each of the beast's heads in Joachim's understanding was an eruption of evil from the entire body of corruption, and Roger de Hoveden explicitly stated that Joachim saw the number seven as a figure representing totality, rather than a literal sum, "something finite for what is infinite" (*The Annals of Roger de Hoveden*, 178). Each head in its own way revealed evil for what it was, so that seven represented the comprehensive cycle of evil's disclosure. Further, Joachim understood in the tradition of Tyconius that the Revelation of John proceeds by recapitulating itself, not in a linear fashion. Nonetheless, seven is a number as well as a symbol, and Joachim wrongly predicted that Richard would celebrate victory just seven years after the capture of Jerusalem. In his reckoning, the antichrist would emerge *soon* thereafter.

When the seven heads had run their course, there would be a rest of a thousand years—a symbolic number in Joachim's thought as in Augustine's. This will be an entirely new state of existence, governed by the Holy Spirit. At that point, evil will have depleted all of its vast resources, as Joachim predicted in his *Book of Figures*, a richly illustrated work:

> Many impious kings and false prophets and antichrists precede the one Antichrist who will pretend to be king and priest and prophet. . . . Yet after the downfall of this Antichrist there will be justice on earth and the abundance of peace; and the Lord will rule from sea to sea and from the river to the ends of the earth. . . . The Jews too and many infidel peoples will be converted to the Lord and the whole population will delight in the beauty of peace. For the heads of the great dragon will be crushed down, and the dragon itself will be imprisoned in the abyss.[4]

Joachim's imagination was visually charged, and he supervised the production of illustrations for his oracular project.

Did Joachim actually show Richard I a picture of the seven-headed dragon? That remains a matter of dispute.[5] Although Joachim's commitment to the pictorial representation of his thought cannot be doubted, his meeting with Richard I came well before the completion of his project. Whether or not Joachim had access to the picture of the seven-headed dragon that has become emblematic of his work as a whole, Roger de Hoveden leaves no doubt about the vivid, visual impression that the oracular prophet made on the king.

A crucial dimension of the prophecy is the quick succession of the sixth to the seventh and final head, the antichrist. Who might this be? Joachim was not specific, yet he remained urgent in his expectation, because he said that the antichrist "is now born in Rome and will be lifted up to the apostolic seat." That reference to Rome might conceivably have appealed to Richard, given the bitter dispute of his family with the papacy. A pope had, after all, forced Richard's father Henry to do penance for complicity in the death of Thomas à Beckett.

But whatever Richard made of this prophecy, for Joachim, "Rome" did not stand for the church. In his worldview, the church was *Jerusalem*, while worldly Rome was Babylon; his prophecy of the antichrist was of a usurper, an anti-pope. After that seventh head had come and gone, Joachim's period of peace would ensue, followed at last by the eruption of "Gog," the tail of the beast, the last effulgence of evil, which finally is consigned to permanent oblivion (Rev 20:7-10).

On this oracular reading, the Revelation of John permitted Joachim to access the inner meaning of Scripture as a whole. By seeing Joachim's approach in its time and observing both its impact and reactions against it, we can appreciate another principal turn in the whole assessment of the meaning of apocalyptic expectation, as well as of the Revelation.

Joachim of Fiore's Two Testaments and Three Divine Status

Joachim's meeting in 1184 with Pope Lucius III came at a fateful time for him, not only in view of the papal support he received, but also within his own development as a commentator and a visionary. He had been planning to write two closely related works. In the first—an encyclopedic *Book of the Harmony of the New Testament and the Old*—he would show the deep affinity between the Testaments, so that, for example, the twelve tribes of Israel corresponded to twelve churches: the seven churches addressed in the Revelation together with the great churches of Rome, Constantinople,

Alexandria, Antioch, and Jerusalem. A second opus was intended as a commentary on the Revelation with its signature vision of the seven seals. Joachim's plans for these concordant volumes put him in the position to speak as he did to Pope Lucius in regard to the capture of Jerusalem, and then to King Richard in regard to his crusade, confident that he had found the inner system that related the events of past, present, and future.

Yet Joachim had hesitated to begin his ambitious project, caught in a monastic catch-22. He wanted to associate his monastery with the Cistercian Order, because he believed that monastic contemplation (and the Cistercians in particular) fulfilled prophecies in the Revelation of John. But, as noted above, the Cistercians did not initially accept the application of the poor monks of Corazzo to join them. Cistercian discipline required Joachim to secure permission to be freed from administration to write; yet how could the Cistercians authorize an activity for a monk they had not accepted? This dilemma explains why Joachim sought papal authorization for his literary monasticism, why it was important for him to show the pope something of his prophetic credentials, and why Lucius' agreement that he should turn from management to parchment marked a pivotal moment in Joachim's life.

The delay in writing proved productive. The hiatus provoked inner turmoil, and a vision. At Pentecost, the spring feast of the Holy Spirit, Joachim reported a visionary experience that was at the same time a conceptual advance. His vision was of a harp in the shape of a triangle. The harp showed him that every event in the Old Testament had its harmonic counterpart in the New Testament, so that while the first Testament represented an actual event, the second Testament more fully disclosed God's purpose.

So far, this confirmed Joachim's revelation on Mount Tabor, although putting it in a more abstract form. The idea of a typology between the Old Testament and the New, such that a figure in Israel's Scriptures referred both to itself and to a fuller realization in the New Testament, had been established many centuries before Joachim. Augustine, for example, related the three divine visitors to Abraham and Sarah under the oaks of Mamre (Gen 18:1-22) to the Holy Trinity (*On the Trinity* 2.11.20).

But the vision of the harp signaled the introduction into Joachim's thought of its new and distinctive element. (He appropriately called the instrument a *psalterium* in Latin, since he was reciting his daily psalms at the time of the vision.) Prior to his prayers he had agonized over the issue of the Trinity, of how divine identity—although unitary—comes down to the three irreducible realities of Father, Son, and Spirit. The harp permitted him to see that the harmonic concordance between the Old Testament and the New Testament could occur because each string or event was strung on the *triangular* harp. One string cannot resonate with another unless it is set at the right distance as well as measuring the appropriate length. An arrangement of strings of the correct attributes set at the resonant interval requires a grid with three points of reference. The fulfillment of the Old Testament in the New Testament needs the three dimensions of Father (in the first Testament), Son (in the second Testament), and Spirit (in the relationship between the first and the second).

Father, Son, and Spirit together, God in God's fullness, permitted the analogies and the disclosure of analogies within the Scriptures according to Joachim's thought. Trinity as indelible in God's character permitted the harmony of the two Testaments to be disclosed within human perception. This provided an incentive for Joachim to go ahead with his projects, and to write an additional work based upon the vision.

Joachim linked events between the Old and the New literally and more closely than in many typological approaches. So, for example, he correlated the generations of Israel with those of the church. Yet just as church follows synagogue, so also there emerges a *spiritual* church at the climax of the whole binary pattern in which fulfillment unfolds.

Joachim saw the Father as dominant in the initial recognition of God within the Old Testament. The Son is the principal figure within the New Testament, and from the Father and Son the Spirit proceeds. He used the Latin term *Status*, which refers to basic condition, to speak of the predominance of one or the other: the *Status* of the Father, or the Son, or the Spirit. As one predominates, the other two always remain present. Although human awareness of God progresses, the three *Status* of God persist throughout all time; the whole point of the Trinity—as full divine being—is that God is Father, Son, *and* Spirit eternally, no matter what people might or might not perceive of the Trinity.

One of the basic affirmations of the theologians who championed Trinitarian orthodoxy was that there was no time when the Son did not exist (as Alexander of Alexandria said in his *Epistle on Arianism* 1.4) and the same characterization applied to the Holy Spirit in this understanding. Joachim adhered strictly and fiercely to this characteristic tenet of orthodoxy.

Because this understanding is essential within Joachim's perspective, he spoke of each *Status* as a basic condition of God, with the Son and the Spirit active with the Father from the very beginning, although one or another predominated. He thought of this as naturally as a scientist recognizes that water remains water whether in a solid, a liquid, or a gaseous state. Spirit does not supersede the Father and the Son, but comes from them, just as the spiritual church proceeds from synagogue and church, and brings with it a spiritual intelligence (*spiritus intelligentiae* or *spiritualis intellectus*). Three kinds of people—married patriarchs, celibate clergy, and contemplative monks—correspond to the three *Status* of God; they are human analogues of divinity, and each predominates according to the *Status* that has emerged.

In reading the Revelation as the model of human experience until his time and thereafter, Joachim committed himself to patterns of recapitulation—but also to patterns of progress. The true meaning of events in Israel could only be known as fulfilled in the experience of the church, and their full significance awaited the disclosure of God's Spirit. That disclosure, the *Status* of the Spirit, comes *after* the antichrist, yet *before* Gog. The Spirit of God constitutes the condition of illumination in the millennium, which becomes the pause between the revelation of history's meaning and the end of history itself. It corresponds to the half hour of blessed, heavenly silence when the seventh seal is opened in Revelation 8:1.

Understanding Joachim's approach necessitates appreciating the distinction between the two Testaments, a fulfillment over time of Scripture's typological meaning, and the three *Status*, which refer at base to the conditions of God's being in the Trinity. The two Testaments refer to anthropological reality, while the three *Status* concern divine reality. To understand Joachim's thinking, Testaments and *Status* cannot be confused with one another. The Son was with the Father and the Holy Spirit *always*, even prior to creation, and all three will be the true temple of the new Jerusalem prophesied by John of Patmos: the awareness of God in the hearts and minds of his people. But over time, which is the only way that people as temporal beings live, the two Testaments range over—and properly interpreted, they explain—the whole of human history from creation until final judgment. The Revelation of John provides the key to Joachim's detailed typology.

During the patriarchal *Status* of the Father, symbolized by Abraham, the Son was present in Isaac, and the Spirit in Jacob; the three archetypical patriarchs signaled God's triune nature. Once Joachim established that correspondence in his mind, he could also spin through the patriarchs as representing *differing* persons of the Trinity, as if in a kaleidoscope.

In fact, Joachim conceives of the second *Status*—that of the Son—as reflected eight centuries *before* Jesus' birth, from the time of King Uzziah during the eighth century BCE; in the year of that monarch's death, the prophet Isaiah had his vision of the triune God in the temple (Isa 6:1-5). So began a period of the *germinatio* (sprouting) of the second *Status* in history, which reached its *fructificatio* (fruit-bearing) in the case of Jesus. Overlaps in the eternal Trinity are mirrored in the overlaps of historical experience.

Likewise, the Spirit has never been absent since the first moment of creation (Gen 1:1), although the Spirit's full accessibility awaits the last breath of history itself. Joachim was fiercely committed to the belief that the Spirit proceeded from both the Father *and the Son*. As recited in the Latin churches, the phrase "and the Son" (*filioque*) was inserted into the text of the Nicene Creed, commonly recited in both East and West, while in the Greek Creed the Spirit was said to proceed simply from the Father. For Joachim, the proud Latinist, this meant that the Spirit dawned both in the *Status* of the Father *and* in the *Status* of the Son.

Elijah the prophet, during the first *Status*, typified the Spirit, so that when he engaged in his prophetic battle on Mount Carmel, the twelve stones of the altar he built signaled the apostles, the earth he dug stood for the Old Testament, the water he poured out symbolized the New Testament, and the fire that miraculously consumed his sacrifice was the *spiritualis intellectus* that Joachim urgently predicted was to be poured out upon humanity as a whole (1 Kgs 18:16-46).[6]

That new effulgence of Spirit, in turn, breaks through during the second *Status* of the Son, according to Joachim in the emergence of a contemplative monastic order under St. Benedict (during the sixth century CE). That brings the prospect of "spiritual men" (*viri spirituales*) fully illuminated in the half hour of silence after the seventh seal is opened, when millennial awareness precedes the final end of evil. The Cistercian reform of the Benedictine rule was yet another advance according to Joachim. The whole of his life was dedicated to the realization of the *Status* of the Holy Spirit during history's final lap of honor. The Cistercians for him were not just an order, but also a vehicle of the Holy Spirit in history. Joining them was not a matter of convenience, but of apocalyptic realization.

Although Father, Son, and Spirit are all and each eternal, perception of them unfolds over time. That unfolding involves overlaps, and Joachim often depicts the three states as intersecting circles. The three, however, are not separate ages (*aetates*) or times (*tempora*), but are indeed *Status*. Although a later interpretation would make Joachim into a prophet of three "ages," that is not accurate. There were two ages, corresponding to two Testaments in his thought, and three *Status*, corresponding to the Trinity and to the human capacity to understand God, as the ages of typology and fulfillment advanced.

Joachim of Fiore's intellectual project, despite the fact that he no more predicted the abortive muddle of Richard I's crusade than he forecast the climax of historical experience, marks a permanent advance beyond the usual view of salvation history. Instead of linear progression, Joachim depicted repeated recapitulation in history, with progress embedded not in the nature of events but in the unfolding perception of the reality of God. The last moment before the end of all things, the half hour of silence after the seventh seal is opened, therefore becomes a beat of time before eternity, when near the close of two Testaments the reality of the three divine *Status* is known. Even when history appears to *regress*, the underlying pulse of awareness grows toward its fruition. Joachim's genius was to discover hope implicit, even within the apparent reversals of history, through the lens of the Revelation's seven seals.

"The One That Restrains"
Contesting Joachim's Vision

Even as he recorded Joachim's discussion with Richard I, Roger de Hoveden contradicted Joachim's reading of the Revelation of John. Roger first invokes the authority of the bishops and other ecclesiastical figures present at the interview with Richard, and then relates their apocalyptic scenario in opposition to Joachim's.

This scenario represents what Roger de Hoveden took to be the consensus from which Joachim wrongly departed. The alternative Roger approves shows that, at the time of Joachim's fateful interview with Richard I, the Revelation was being understood in ways that neither Papias nor Augustine could have predicted, that moved in a different direction from Joachim's, but that also saw the text in oracular terms.

Roger de Hoveden follows a traditional interpretation of the Apocalypse that Hippolytus pioneered in the third century, and predicts that the antichrist shall be born of the Jews. Specifically, he will fulfill the prophecy that Dan, the son of Jacob and founder of the Israelite clan that carries his name, will dominate Israel (Gen 49:16). This apparently strange descent could claim some support from the Revelation, since Dan is *not* listed in the count of the 144,000 from Israel who are sealed for salvation (Rev 7). Further, Jacob had said that his son Dan would be a serpent (Gen 49:17). By the Middle Ages, the serpent was a stable symbol of Satan, and had all but lost its ancient association with wisdom.[7]

Descended from the tribe of Dan, Roger de Hoveden's antichrist will nonetheless be born in Babylon, the source of eschatological evil according to the Revelation of John (chapter 17). Although born in Babylon, he will be brought up in Bethsaida and Chorazin, to fulfill Jesus' prophecies against those places (Matt 11:21; Luke 10:13). Then, armed with magic arts, the antichrist will ensconce himself in Jerusalem, rebuild the Jewish temple, circumcise himself, and attempt, by bribery and persecution, to destroy the work of Christ.

By the time of Roger, the characterization of Jews as representing the synagogue of Satan had taken hold. Describing the crowning of Richard the Lionhearted in 1189, the chronicle of Richard of Devizes offers an account that is as chilling in its rhetoric as the atrocities against Jews in England that it praises were inhuman. The chronicle refers to the Eucharist that solemnized the coronation as the sacrifice of Christ, linking that sacrifice to another, and the slaughter by Christian mobs of Jews described as "vermin":

> On the very day of the coronation, about that solemn hour, in which the Son was immolated to the Father, a sacrifice of the Jews to their father the devil was commenced in the city of London, and so long was the duration of this famous mystery, that the holocaust could scarcely be accomplished the ensuing day.[8]

Roger de Hoveden and other chroniclers of his time reflect an attitude that stands in contrast to Joachim's prediction of a time of Jewish conversion. Their visions seem surreal, but for differing reasons. Joachim of Fiore systematizes the whole of Scripture with his Trinitarian reading, using the Revelation as the lens of his system, while Roger de Hoveden aggregates diverse biblical references in the service of a substantially new narrative, an eschatological adventure of what is to happen at the end of times.

In aggregating previous authorities Roger de Hoveden's apocalypse even claims that its idiosyncratic scenario derives from an apocryphal prophecy attributed to John of Patmos. That is the alleged source of the antichrist's nativity from Dan and his upbringing in Chorazin and Bethsaida. Such a narrative is completely foreign to the Revelation of John. One of the ironies of influence is that high esteem, which the Revelation enjoyed during the Middle Ages, brings attributions to works that have nothing to do with their original or intended meanings.

Throughout his description Roger de Hoveden develops a detailed emphasis on the mirror image of symmetry between Christ and the antichrist, usually citing or alluding to biblical passages by way of support. The antichrist in his new temple, says Roger, *produces* the great tribulation that Jesus predicted in the Gospels (Matt 24:15-28; Mark 13:14-23; Luke 21:20-24). The original texts make no mention of the antichrist as the agent of this destruction; the travails depict divine judgment, not demonic chaos. But once the content of the antichrist could be filled in from the beast in the Revelation, the way was open to make him an ever more fearsome figure. By bringing passages together that were initially independent, in this case concerning the antichrist and the great tribulation, Roger's apocalypse creates an innovative plot out of scriptural and apocryphal elements. It gives the impression of traditional belief, but in fact constitutes a new narrative.

Roger de Hoveden's apocalypse usually deploys scriptural language without citation, leaving the reader to infer the books and passages involved, but it concludes with a specific and emphatic reference to Paul's Second Letter to the Thessalonians. In that letter, an antichrist-like figure is referred to as "the son of perdition" (2:3), who is barely held in check by "what restrains" (2:6).[9] Then, still relying on reference to 2 Thessalonians, Roger de Hoveden's apocalypse introduces the crucial feature of its perspective, which differentiates it from Joachim's root and branch: *in Roger's view and in the view of the apocalypse he quotes, the millennium cannot start as long as the Roman Empire lasts.* Even though diminished, the empire continues in the kingdom of the Franks, and the antichrist is held in check until the imperial line comes to an end. Only after that will the final tribulation be unleashed.

In direct contrast to Joachim, Roger wants to show how history in its present form continues, rather than closes with a transition to a new *Status* before the end. If the Roman Empire can be perpetuated, then divine judgment, although inevitable, can be forestalled. In accepting this view, Roger draws upon a reading of the Revelation some millenarians held that had been current since the second century. The second-century church father Tertullian, for example, also turned to 2 Thessalonians and assumed that Paul's mention of the phrase "what restrains" refers to the Roman Empire.[10] Millenarians, of course, anticipated the eclipse of the Roman Empire; medieval apocalyptists had other ideas.

Once the connection between "what restrains" and the Roman Empire was made, it could be used after the time of Constantine *in support of the Roman Empire.* After all, the antichrist is not referred to in 2 Thessalonians 2:6. That means that the reference to "what restrains" in 2 Thessalonians can become a promise that the world will be *as enduring as* the Roman Empire. In a stunning reversal of Tertullian's interpretation that reflects the force of the Constantinian settlement, this is just what John Chrysostom, an ardently symbolic millenarian who died in 407 CE, argued.[11] The Christianized Empire had become the principle that *preserves* the world as we know it, the reason to cherish the status quo rather than to anticipate its end.

Roger de Hoveden's apocalypse did not need to be directly aware of Chrysostom in order to refer to the importance of the Roman Empire in giving humanity respite before the millennium and the final end of the world. This claim also featured in French royal propaganda for Philip Augustus,[12] so that Roger represents an establishment mainstream of medieval consensus. The same winter that Richard I met Joachim in Messina, Frederick Barbarossa died of drowning on his way to liberate Jerusalem. He had been motivated to take the cross by a scenario very much like Roger's. Claims comparable to those made for Philip Augustus pushed Frederick, as Holy Roman Emperor, to restore the balance between this world and the next, in order to delay the end of the world.[13]

By the time of Roger and Joachim, although the millennium continued to be seen as the rule of the saints prior to Christ's definitive advent to judge the world, a signal shift had occurred in the Augustinian understanding of the Revelation. Instead of assuming that a political millennium had already begun, many theologians now anticipated one in the future. The break up of the Roman

Empire in the West, the rise of Islam, and in particular the Muslim conquest of Jerusalem were too much for many Christian thinkers to reconcile with Augustine's claim that the rule of the saints had truly been established. Joachim eagerly expected the millennium, while Roger's authorities hoped to put it off until the Roman Empire had done all the good it possibly could. Both approaches, however, implicitly departed from Augustinian teaching.

History and Apocalypse

By the twelfth century, the meaning of the Revelation had changed.[14] It was neither principally the anticipation of the millennium, as it was for Papias, nor the celebration of the millennium, as it was for Augustine. Rather, the purpose of the book and all apocalyptic thinking was to relate events in current time to the unfolding pattern of salvation as a whole. The Revelation of John became a lexicon for those in the Middle Ages who strove to explain why great Christian regimes were rising and falling, and what that meant for the future.

They awaited the millennium instead of celebrating its coming. Even Byzantine interpreters had lost confidence that they were living during the thousand-year reign of the saints. In the words of an Eastern apocalyptic prediction that appeared in 692 CE,[15] the reign of a last Byzantine ruler would defeat the Muslim "Ishmaelites," and usher in "the last peace and perfection of the world." This "King of the Greeks" would also deal with the warring nations of Gog and Magog, and place his crown on the true cross, which he would restore to its place on Golgotha after rescuing it from its Muslim captors. Then "immediately the True Cross will be raised to heaven, and the King of the Greeks will give up his soul to his creator and immediately every leader and every authority and all powers will cease" (*Revelations of the Pseudo-Methodius* 14.8).

Byzantine apocalypses, although fed by imagery from the Revelation, clearly went their own oracular way into military and political forecasts. The same source also, long before Roger de Hoveden, identified the antichrist with Dan.[16] In Roger de Hoveden's case, Gog is identified with the Jews, and this helps to explain why his antichrist is emphatically Jewish: centered on the temple, practicing circumcision, seeking to force Christians to betray their faith. At the same time, Jewish eschatological thought is also an influence on Roger's apocalypse, because the Messiah in rabbinic sources of this period was clearly expected to rebuild the temple, establish the law of Moses, and punish Gentiles. Chapter 53 of the book of Isaiah, for example, is devoted in the Aramaic rendering available during the Middle Ages to a depiction of the complete dominance of the Messiah, whose work is crowned by the reestablishment of the temple.[17] The tradition Roger represents absorbed such Jewish expectations into its creative and anti-Semitic depiction of the antichrist.

In contrast, Joachim's view of the future is that it will be a time, neither of Byzantine victory nor of the Jewish antichrist, but of Jewish conversion. Gog is no longer a people, but a symbol of the corruption that is to be overcome. Key to this new view is Joachim's optimistic conviction, as compared to Roger's, that the millennium brings, not disaster, but the release of God's Spirit upon all humanity.

Developments in Muslim apocalypses during this period also reflect the use of the Revelation as part of oracular prophecy. These works are frequently referred to under the name of Daniel, but their additions are often creative, and in some cases key contributions come from the Revelation. For example, in the *Kitab al-malahim* of Ibn-Mundai,[18] a work current from the tenth century, a quasi-messianic figure called the Sufyani confronts the true Messiah, descended from the Prophet, the Husani. Their confrontation is followed by the defeat of the antichrist by al-Khidr (an ancient prophet) and by Jesus. This introduces a messianic kingdom guided by descendants of al-Hasan and al-Husayn (the two grandsons of the Prophet). Finally, the war of Gog and Magog brings an end to all things. The influence of the Revelation is palpable in the invocation of Jesus among several prophetic figures, and in the ratcheting up of violence until Gog and Magog.

Joachim's Trinitarian orientation sets him apart from Muslim interpretations that drew on the Revelation, and the desire to prolong this world, the consensus view that Roger de Hoveden represents, did not control Joachim's vision any more than dreams of Byzantine military victory did. Yet across the board, the oracular reading of the Revelation prompted a sense that current events had become apocalyptic events.

Ibn-Mundai's apocalypse is filled with realistic descriptions. This interweaving of current and apocalyptic events also characterized the oracular approach of the crusaders.[19] A chronicler of the First Crusade could refer to the blood on the Temple Mount reaching to the horses' bridles in a way that imitated the Revelation's image of blood flowing out of the winepress of God's wrath to the depth of horses' bridles (14:20).

For all the violence of these images, an apocalyptic approach such as Roger de Hoveden's offered the prospect of forestalling the end. Joachim of Fiore was unusual among Christian interpreters in actively seeking and seeing signs of its coming. Joachim influenced later developments as the Revelation's most celebrated commentator, but Roger remains the more representative medieval thinker. Aggregation is more important than system in Roger de Hoveden's apocalypse, and time is afforded on earth to work out divine justice in all its detail, much as during the same period purgatory needed to find its way into the other side of history in order to right the consequences of the flawed but divine longings of humanity.[20] God's ordered justice, a characteristic preoccupation of medieval thinkers at many levels, needed time to be worked out on earth, as in heaven. Joachim found himself in a brilliant minority, but a minority nonetheless.

The enthusiasm for history's climax, nurtured by a reading of the Revelation and keen for its quick arrival, would only prove in the time after Joachim to surpass the traditional, medieval apocalypse of Roger de Hoveden. But the gentle, reclusive monk wound up provoking waves of militant zeal, from which Europe took long to recover, and some say never recovered. That development arose from an interpretation of Joachim's approach that he never saw coming.

Further Reading

Joachim is a complex thinker whose work has been analyzed extensively. See Henri de Lubac, *La Postérité spirituelle de Joachim de Flore*, Le Sycomore, Série Horizon 3.8 (Paris: Lethielleux, 1979, 1981); E. Randolph Daniel, *Abbot Joachim of Fiore: Liber de Concordia Noui ac Veteris Testamenti*, Transactions of the American Philosophical Society 73.8 (Philadelphia: American Philosophical Society, 1983); Bernard McGinn, *The Calabrian Abbot: Joachim of Fiore in the History of Western Thought* (New York: Macmillan, 1985); Marjorie Reeves, *Joachim of Fiore & the Prophetic Future: A Medieval Study in Historical Thinking* (Stroud, U.K.: Sutton, 1999); idem, *The Figurae of Joachim of Fiore*, Oxford-Warburg Studies (Oxford: Clarendon, 1972); Matthias Riedl, *Joachim von Fiore: Denker der vollendeten Menschheit* (Würzburg: Koenigshausen & Neumann, 2004); and Robert E. Lerner, "Antichrists and Antichrist in Joachim of Fiore," *Speculum* 60.3 (1985): 553–70.

4

War with the Antichrist

> War happened in heaven, with Michael and his angels fighting against the dragon, and the dragon and *his* angels fought. And he did not prevail, nor was a place found for them in heaven. And the great dragon was thrown—that ancient serpent called the devil and Satan who deceives the whole world—was thrown to the earth, and his angels were thrown with him.
>
> Revelation 12:7-9

Antagonists in many theological disputes during the thirteenth century believed that their opponents were worse than wrong; they characterized opposition as the embodiment of evil, as the antichrist. The depiction of adversaries as incarnations of Satan often imitated Joachim of Fiore's identification of the dragon's seven heads.

Those who drew from Joachim's reading of the Revelation during the thirteenth century and later did more than speculate on the identity of the antichrist. They were also keen to identify the truly "spiritual men" (as Joachim called them, *viri spirituales*), who exceeded all other human agents in holiness and authority. In their eyes, the war in heaven described in the Revelation of John had been joined on earth; their opponents represented the antichrist on earth *while they alone were on the side of the angels* in the dawning *Status* of the Holy Spirit.

These apocalyptic militants, who believed that heaven's war had come to earth in the last moment prior to God's definitive intervention in history, saw themselves as the advance guard of divine judgment against the antichrist. They felt compelled to take up spiritual battle, and for that purpose if necessary real battle, with the force of arms. Use of the Revelation in order to identify both heaven's warriors and the minions of Satan became current during the Middle Ages, but has never disappeared since then.

This metaphysical polarization, intensified by Joachim's influence, became a constant and growing presence in Christian thought during the centuries leading up to the Reformation. Fifty years after Joachim's death, a Franciscan teacher named Gerardo di Borgo San Donnino published a commentary on Joachim's writings called *Introduction to the Eternal Gospel* (1254). This approach made Joachim himself into an apocalyptic messenger predicted by the Revelation.

Gerardo identified *Joachim's writings* as the eternal gospel that John of Patmos had in mind when he said in Revelation 14:6-7:

> And I saw another angel flying in midheaven, having an eternal gospel to announce over those dwelling on the earth—even over every nation and tribe and language and people, saying in a great voice, Fear God and give him glory, because the hour of his judgment has come, and worship him who made the heaven and the earth, and sea and springs of water.

According to Gerardo, Joachim was that angel, and his preaching superseded both the Old and New Testaments in the third and final *Status* of the Holy Spirit.This interpretation was influenced by Origen's reading of Revelation 14:6-7, which found in the passage a prediction of a new, spiritual understanding of Christ's teaching and actions,but its claims for Joachim's inspiration were radical and unprecedented.[1]

Joachim had made no such claim of divine supersession on his own behalf. Yet he did teach that the third *Status* opened an epoch of contemplative monasticism, grounded in Spirit and bringing to fruition all earlier attempts at communion with God. Gerardo's reading of Joachim went further. The rise of the Franciscan movement after Joachim's death inspired Gerardo's conception.

As he read the Revelation of John, Francis of Assisi was also an angel, the angel of the sixth seal in Revelation 6:12-17. The result was to portray the saint, not as the gentle-to-animals pantheist of some modern depictions, but as a key figure of apocalyptic fury.

When the sixth seal is opened in the vision of John of Patmos, the powerful on earth are crushed:

> And the kings of the earth and the magnates and the generals and the rich and the powerful and every servant and free person hid themselves in the caves and in the rocks of the mountains. And they say to the mountains and to the rocks, Fall upon us and hide us from the face of the one who sits upon the Throne and from the wrath of the Lamb. Because the great day of their wrath has come, and who is able to stand? (Rev 6:15-16)

This was to be the dawn of the poor, identified by Gerardo di Borgo San Donnino as those Franciscans who upheld the commitment to poverty of St. Francis against the compromise of those in the order who accepted the conventions of this world.

In Gerardo's bold amalgam of vision and exegesis, the spiritual men—exemplified by Francis of Assisi (1181–1226) and predicted by Joachim (1135–1202)—were to replace the world rule of the hierarchical church. Taken together, John of Patmos, Joachim of Fiore, and Francis of Assisi provided Gerardo with a template of prophetic transition, revolution, and millennial realization.

Gerardo also read key passages in the Revelation in order to determine just when the rule of the poor was to begin, proceeding on the assumption, pervasive during his period (as it had been before and would be after his time), that the "days" mentioned in the Revelation are really years. In the Revelation, chapter 12, the woman, who must be the church (as Gerardo agreed with many other commentators), flees into the wilderness and is protected from the seven-headed dragon for a total of 1,260 days (Rev 12:6). Then a war breaks out in heaven that heralds Satan's consignment to the pit and the thousand-year rule of those who reign with Christ: these are Joachim's spiritual men according to Gerardo. The association of images, numbers, and patterns made it obvious to Gerardo and his supporters that the millennial reign of the spiritual Franciscans would begin in the year 1260.

All other claimants to authority, including the papacy, would correspondingly disappear from the scene, buried under the mountains that fall with the opening of the sixth seal, while Satan himself was to be consigned to the pit for a thousand years (Rev 20:2-3). Gerardo made Joachim into a literalist millenarian; the third *Status* now became a new temporal age, whose coming followed an apocalyptic calendar.

The year after the publication of Gerardo's *Introduction to the Eternal Gospel,* Pope Alexander set up a commission of cardinals to condemn the work. The book was burned and its recalcitrant author later put in prison, where he died in 1276. The head of the Franciscans, John of Parma (1209–1289), was for his part deposed for supporting Gerardo and continuing to esteem Joachim's teaching despite its increased association with attacks on the papacy.

Official persecution did not, however, deter those who looked to Joachim's teaching for inspiration. Indeed, resistance encouraged the spiritual Franciscans to solidify into a faction dedicated to preserving Francis' original style of poverty and charismatic guidance against the blandishments and threats of worldly power. Once an opponent is branded as the antichrist, and his actions illustrated with the imagery of the Revelation, his increasing opposition is bound to be taken as proof that he truly is to be identified with evil.

Franciscan opposition to the papacy threatened the stability of Christendom, and some of the best minds of the Middle Ages attempted to resolve the problem by conciliation. John of Parma's successor as minister general of the Franciscans, St. Bonaventure (1217–1274), moderated his order's support of Joachim's position. Bonaventure insisted *against* Gerardo that the New Testament is itself eternal and not to be superseded. Yet Bonaventure also embraced Joachim's theory of concordances between the Old Testament and the New Testament, and popularized the identification of St. Francis with the angel of the sixth seal. This was a key endorsement of reading the Revelation as prophesying Francis, the herald of a new age of Spirit.

Bonaventure deftly deflected criticism that came the Franciscans' way for Gerardo's delegitimation of the papacy. Instead of equating the antichrist with the pope, he targeted those who in his judgment misused the philosophy of Aristotle, rivals at the University of Paris. At the same time, Bonaventure avoided a war of apocalyptic rhetoric between his own Franciscans and the Dominicans, making a joint statement with them that claimed an apocalyptic role for *both* orders, in language reminiscent of Joachim's, "In these latest of days at the end of the ages."[2] He maintained the rhetoric of apocalyptic warfare, even as he protected church authority from identification with the antichrist.

Not all Franciscans embraced Bonaventure's learned and diplomatic attempt to reconcile Joachim's thought with conventional scholasticism in support of the papacy. Some Franciscans agreed enthusiastically that St. Francis was the angel of the sixth seal, but that meant that Gerardo was right: Joachim had announced a new, eternal gospel, just as the Revelation forecast (14:6). The rule of spiritual men was about to replace, not academic opponents, but the power of wealth (Rev 6:15-17) in kingdoms and principalities—the papacy included.

Growing animosity split the "Spirituals," who held to Francis' tenets of charismatic poverty, from the "Conventuals," who lived in communities under the jurisdiction of the pope. This schism dominated Franciscan life well beyond the period of the Middle Ages and into the Reformation. Their rivalry made the antichrist, whose portrait was painted on the basis of the Revelation, into a deeply divisive symbol.

One spiritual Franciscan, Petrus Olivi (who died in 1298), insisted that a strict application of Francis' rule meant identifying both the papacy and the Holy Roman Empire with the antichrist. In that same tradition, Ubertino de Casale (1259–1329) identified the first beast of Revelation 13 with Pope Boniface VIII and the second beast of that chapter with Pope Benedict XI.[3] These interpretations of the Revelation via Joachim and Gerardo provided the reforming discourse with one of its most potent theological and rhetorical antipapal arguments centuries *before* the Protestant Reformation itself. In fact, contemporaries of Olivi's announced that they would lead the *reformatio* of the church in order to restore its intended poverty and spirituality.

The power of the papacy had increased steadily during the thirteenth century. The authority to declare a crusade was used against Christians in the south of France (the Cathars), clerical celibacy and obedience to the pope were enforced, and confession of sin to a priest was made a requirement of all Catholics. Yet even growing papal influence proved unequal to the task of suppressing the conviction, grounded in Joachim's reading of the Revelation, that Christendom was on the cusp of a breakthrough of millennial proportions.

The Franciscan Nicholas of Lyra found a way during the fourteenth century, as had Bonaventure before him, to reconcile Francis' teaching with the authority of Rome. He explained in his *Commentary on the Apocalypse* (1329) that John of Patmos had predicted the whole of the history of the church by means of his visions. He made the Revelation into a map of the past and a guide for the future, so that history proceeded by means of apocalyptic necessity. This world had become the battleground of heaven.

Crucially, Nicholas of Lyra articulated the principle in interpretation of a *double* literal sense within the Scriptures: prophets speak both for their own times and for what is to come.[4] This refinement of Joachim's search for concordances also enabled Nicholas to insist that, although not a prophet himself, he could nonetheless interpret those chapters of the Revelation that dealt with the past. Insofar as the Revelation concerns the *future*, however (particularly from chapter 17 in his view, to which history had not yet caught up), Nicholas called for caution. He insisted that one needed to be aware that, while John of Patmos was a prophet, the interpreter of his text is not. Even as he followed Bonaventure in *not* proclaiming the Franciscans to be the agents who will fulfill the millennium, Nicholas continued an apocalyptic reading of history that related the heavenly images of the text to events on earth. He acknowledged uncertainty in regard to the future, yet he provided the basis to hope the time would enable future events, once they occurred, to find their sense in the images of the Revelation. Although this represents a critical refinement of Joachim's approach, its indebtedness to him is evident.

A similar perspective plays through Dante's *Divine Comedy*, composed just before the appearance of Nicholas' *Commentary*. Dante lovingly depicts Joachim as "the Calabrian abbot Joachim, endowed with prophetic spirit" (*Paradiso* 12.139–41).[5] Siding with the supporters of Joachim, Dante joins in the apocalyptic critique of the papacy as making the church into the whore of Revelation 17 (*Inferno* 19.106–17) and in the consignment of Pope Boniface VIII to hell (19.52–57). With Dante, a militant application of Joachim's approach entered the mainstream of thought and sensibility. The Revelation of John had become, if not a precise handbook for reform, then at least a motivation to confront the beast that had invaded the Catholic Church.

Martin Luther's Apocalyptic Conversion

Although the Reformation would, over time, hammer the text of the Revelation into a blunt instrument against the papacy, when Martin Luther published a preface to the Revelation in 1522 at an early stage of his career, he showed a distinct lack of enthusiasm for the text. Fresh from his disputes concerning the true basis of faith and practice, which he found in the writings of Paul above all, Luther struck a dismissive attitude, complaining that "my spirit cannot abide this book." He did not see the teaching of Christ clearly reflected in it. How could he, when—as he complained—the images of the book are diffuse to the point of obscurity? Luther stated rather testily in this preface, citing Revelation 22:7 ("Blessed is he who keeps the words of the prophecy of this scroll"), that "they will be blessed who keep what is written in it, but no one knows what that is, let alone how to keep it."[6]

A scant eight years later, however, Luther published a new and profound appreciation for the Revelation of John, finding within it the resources to attack the principal faults of the church, and therefore to clear the way for the true gospel. In this much more influential preface to the Revelation, brought out in 1530, Luther sharpened the by-then traditional critique of the papacy. Instead of targeting particular pontiffs, he went much farther, attacking the whole "papal empire and the imperial papacy," which he defined as the arrogation by the pope of secular as well as spiritual power.[7]

In this light, the two beasts of Revelation's chapter 13 became for Luther the twin papal pretensions to secular and spiritual authority. Luther accused the papacy of filling the world with the superstitions (as he saw them) that were his pet peeves—"monasteries, foundations, saints, pilgrimages, purgatory, indulgences, celibacy, and innumerable human doctrines and works," not to mention wars of papal instigation. To his mind, these were examples of "all kinds of idolatry," the emblematic blasphemy of Revelation—the worship of the beast (13:4-18). Against that power, the force of the gospel is greater, as Christ and his saints (the Lamb and his throng in Rev 14 and 15) stand opposed to those who cling to the papacy.[8] Those remaining in thrall to the beast are thrown outside the city of Christ and condemned to the wrath of God.

In his preface of 1530 Luther firmly placed himself and his followers within the apocalyptic scenario of the last times as instruments of Armageddon, not merely observers. The papacy was the penultimate woe of Christendom. The Saracens had already been faced, and once the papacy was dispatched there would be only the last remaining woe, Gog and Magog, whom Luther identified as "the Turks and the red Jews," that is, the preeminent Muslim power along with a mythical Jewish race that, it was believed, would appear at the end of time to engage in battle.[9] According to this apocalyptic reading, the Reformation brought all of history not merely to the millennial reign of the saints, but beyond that—to its complete end at the final judgment of Christ.

The Revelation of John for Luther represents the assurance that "no force or lies, no wisdom or holiness, no tribulation or suffering will suppress Christendom."[10] This confidence in both the corruption of his papal opponents and the righteousness of the gospel's cause within a reading of the Revelation helps explain the militancy of Luther's religious revolution. At Luther's funeral, Johann Bugenhagen compared his colleague to the angel with the eternal gospel in Revelation 14:6-7.[11] That angel announced judgment, rather than triumph alone.

By the time Luther came to write his second preface, he had experienced firsthand the militant zeal of millennial readings of the Revelation. He also knew how easily they could turn against him and lead to violence. In 1525 his pamphlet *Against the Robbing and Murdering Hordes of Peasants*, came out in favor of a forceful suppression of the religiously motivated Peasants' War of 1524–1525. Although he urged rulers to exercise discretion in their use of military power, Luther sanctioned the deaths of tens of thousands of people with arguments such as this one:

> Thus it may be that one who is killed fighting on the ruler's side may be a true martyr in the eyes of God, if he fights with such a conscience as I have just described, for he is in God's Word and is obedient to him. On the other hand, one who perishes on the peasants' side is an eternal brand of hell, for he bears the sword against God's Word and is disobedient to him, and is a member of the devil.[12]

Luther knew the enemy he described. One of his followers, a brilliant preacher named Thomas Müntzer (1489–1525), mastered the imagery of the Revelation and turned against Luther. Müntzer framed a powerful rhetoric of political as well as theological revolution from the visions of the Revelation, which *supported* the Peasants' War, and directly opposed his former teacher. For Müntzer, the antichrist was not merely the papacy, but *all* forms of worldly authority.[13] Where Luther—supporting his position with Paul's Letter to the Romans (and particularly chapter 13)—saw the nobility as a social class established by God within the secular realm, even when they did not fully support his reformation, Müntzer was prepared to sanction the use of force at an apocalyptic level to resist what he saw as unjust hierarchy in any form.

According to Müntzer's reading of Revelation 14:14-16, which depicted "one like a son of man having upon his head a gold crown and in his hand a sharp sickle," Jesus was the Son of Man and Müntzer's followers were the sickle. True spirituality required action, the willingness to be the sickle in Jesus' hand. Müntzer's followers were the angelic agents of divine judgment, while Müntzer described himself as one of the two witnesses in Revelation 11. Since the time of Tertullian (*De anima* 50.5), the two witnesses had been identified by some interpreters as Enoch and Elijah. Müntzer believed that he personally had come in the spirit and power of Elijah, and that, together with all those inspired by God's Spirit, he would take part in the divine harvest.

Müntzer repudiated the approach of Luther, which he regarded as academic rather than spiritual. He endorsed a program, not of commentary, but of millennial revolution. The result has been given the name "the Radical Reformation" by historians, an apt designation of the explosive mix of political and theological forces that combined in revolutionary movements such as Müntzer promoted. He insisted that all the elect who participated in the Spirit of God were the true architects of society, and he reached into the meaning of Scripture to articulate his insight. The result was a poetic usage of scriptural language, in which Müntzer brought his followers into the world of the Spirit, as he understood it.[14] This was the inspiration for his using heavenly images taken from the Revelation in order to identify what he and his followers were doing. It also justified Müntzer in his conviction that the concordance between the Revelation and the Old Testament meant that ancient patriarchal practices could be revived for a completely new age.

When some three hundred thousand people rose up against all the authorities that oppressed them—not only the papacy, but also the electors and magistrates of Germany—they proved the motivational power of Müntzer's zeal. Theirs was the greatest popular revolt in Europe until the French Revolution and inspired later uprisings by Anabaptists, a protestant movement committed to adult baptism. Their millennial program found startling concordances in Scripture that Joachim had never described, identifying the reign of the saints not only with the apostles in the practice of common possessions (Acts 4:32-37), but with the patriarchs of Israel in the practice of taking multiple wives. Although Anabaptist claims varied widely, they fundamentally agreed that the apocalyptic Spirit was running through the veins and actions of the elect.

Martin Luther, opposed diametrically and with visceral intensity to the Anabaptists, stressed the power of learning to unlock the meaning of the Scriptures, and the necessity of magistrates to administer God's justice, however imperfectly. His was a call for a "Magisterial Reformation," as historians have called his appeal to duly authorized sources of teaching and justice, distinguishing Luther's views from those of the radical reformers. He emphasized that mortal intellect and human authority were flawed, and yet also portrayed them—as any attentive student of Paul would—as offering a reflection of God's way for humanity. Humanity might now see only through a glass, darkly (1 Cor 13:12), but people do see; governments might err in their assessment of blame, but at least they are established to distinguish good from bad (Rom 13:1-7).

In the end, however, Luther did not content himself with an appeal to the divine approval of magisterial authority. He went beyond that and offered a fresh, Protestant perspective on the Revelation, and on the whole apocalyptic drama of which he believed he was a part. In the new preface of 1530, Luther focuses on the nature of prophecy and establishes a hierarchy of differing kinds of prophecy. His approach rescued the book of Revelation for the Magisterial Reformation and honed powerful rhetorical weapons against both the radical Reformation and the papacy, all the while offering potent tools for influencing how the book would be understood for centuries to come.

Prophecy of the purest and highest kind, maintains Luther, consists of what he believed to be St. Paul's definition: interpreting the *writings* of the prophets.[15] Paul had cited the words of Habakkuk, "The just shall live by faith" (Hab 2:4; cf. Rom 1:17; Gal 3:11), and this principle was Luther's charter. By beginning with this exegetical form of prophecy, rather than any claims of direct inspiration from God, Luther maintained the place of a learned magisterium within the Reformation and fundamentally refuted Thomas Müntzer's perspective. If the basis of prophecy is Scripture rather than direct inspiration, the issues of how meaning is determined will always remain crucial. Intellectual rigor takes the lead from charismatic poetry in the interpretation of the Revelation and of the Scriptures generally in Luther's thought.

Luther names three forms of prophecy that predict the future in various ways, but these are clearly ranked *beneath* exegetical prophecy: prophetic witness to salvation by faith alone takes precedence over the issue of prediction.[16] Predictions can nonetheless offer ancillary support to the truth of the gospel. The first form of predictive prophecy uses words to foreshadow Christ, such as when the Pentateuch refers to God giving manna, miraculous bread in the wilderness; this is then fulfilled by Jesus giving his life (see Exod 16:15; Num 11:7-9; John 6:31-35, 48-51). The second uses images, but also provides interpretation, such as in the book of Daniel, where Daniel sees visions and an angel interprets them. The third consists of images alone, as in the Revelation of John, which makes this form of prophecy the most difficult of all to interpret.

In his preface of 1530 Luther complains that other commentators had used the obscurity of the Revelation's text as an occasion to insert their own "silly notions." He justifies his earlier reluctance to enter into discussion of the work on these grounds. But the text, on this later reading, does refer to future events. Luther contends that the prophecies in the Revelation finally become manifest in a correlation between images in the text that are in the future from the perspective of John of Patmos, but accomplished in events that wise commentators can search out and know in their histories. This approach, inspired by Nicholas of Lyra, leads Luther to frame the entire history of the Catholic Church from the time of the apostles as a fulfillment of the prophetic imagery in the Revelation of John.

Luther equates the Revelation's images of good angels with the greatest past teachers of the church—figures such as Athanasius and those who produced the ancient creeds of the church. The images of trumpets, however, represent evil angels—these are heretics. One kind of heresy is represented in the burning mountain brought forth by the second angel sounding the trumpet in Revelation 8:8. This is false teaching that is not grounded in Scripture, but invents freely and spoils the biblical meaning. Luther names various gnostic groups in this regard—as well as Thomas Müntzer![17] In other words, Luther portrays Müntzer's *failing* in the free poetic usage of the Revelation's language that had been Müntzer's appeal leading up the Peasants' War.

In a bold stroke Luther folded his rival's movement into the text, making Müntzer into one of the trials of the church. At the same time, he upheld the magisterial principle that true prophecy is not merely private illumination, but remains consonant with the exegesis of Scripture.

Luther's approach to the Revelation gives pride of place to the climactic battle with the imperial papacy, which on his reading fulfills the visionary truth of Revelation 13:

> There are now the two beasts (13:1, 11). The first is the empire. The second with the two horns is the papacy, which has now become a temporal power but in the guise of the name of Christ. The pope has reestablished the fallen empire, extending it from the Greeks to the Germans.[18]

Not only does Luther identify the papacy with the beast in Revelation 13, he also describes the angelic figure and its announcement of the eternal gospel in chapter 14 as representing the preaching of the Reformation. Luther further sees the subsequent chapters addressing contemporary events, and speaking to the need for apocalyptic reform, "as the harvest is gathered and those who cling to the papacy against the gospel are thrown outside the city of Christ and into the cold of God's wrath."[19]

Luther does not hesitate to name his papal opponents as the frog-like demons that come out of the beast's mouth (in Rev 16:13), so reducing his inveterate and eloquent disputant, Johann Eck, to the image of a croaky sophist.[20] The whore of Babylon in chapter 17, however, is the more fateful image of a papacy on the verge of collapse, with the punishments of Revelation 18 and the triumph of the Word of God in Revelation 19 just over the horizon of expectation. Gog and Magog lie beyond, as a coda within a triumphant conclusion. For Luther, the Augustinian friar imbued with a sense of the final confrontation between good and evil, the proper focus of expectation was not the millennium of the saints (as in Müntzer), but rather the wars of Gog and Magog that would bring the world to its end.

For all his vehemence in regard to the papacy and Jews, in offering his account of the Revelation's meaning, Luther nonetheless introduced a note of uncertainty. His survey of how images in the text correspond to events in history includes the caveat that these correlations make the interpretation "certain or the least unobjectionable."[21] Between what is certain and what is not objectionable, of course, there is a world of difference. Where Müntzer resorted to arms in order to defend his claim of direct inspiration in reading Scripture as the charter of Christendom, Luther resorted to arms to guard against both Müntzer's heresy and papal corruption, but in the end he could not make his interpretations absolute.

By introducing a degree of uncertainty into the apocalyptic application of the Revelation, over the long term Luther influenced and encouraged those inclined to bring Protestant militancy under control. During Luther's time, in the first flush of the Reformation and the Counter-Reformation (its Catholic counterpart), appeal to apocalyptic rhetoric regularly cast opponents in the role of the antichrist. It was a time when partisans of sometimes aggressively violent movements literally saw themselves as on the side of the angels. It was easy enough for Johann Eck to turn the tables on Luther and accuse him of being a species of antichrist, which he predictably did. Even within the sixteenth century, some Protestant commentators, particularly those associated with Geneva and Zürich, backed away from apocalyptic engagement. John Calvin was particularly trenchant in his treatment of millennialism, which he described as "too puerile to need or deserve refutation."[22] In England, however, even those Puritans who looked to Calvin for guidance in fundamental theology followed the lead of Luther in their enthusiasm for apocalyptic warfare, and pioneered a distinctive theology.

Puritan Calendars of Battle

Even as wars of religion raged in Germany and France, Reformers in England were inspired by apocalyptic rhetoric fueled by the Revelation of John. John Bale, an English friar turned Reformer who published a commentary on the Revelation in 1548, put forward a dualistic perspective. The true church was the heavenly woman of chapter 12 and the "church of hypocrites" was the whore of chapter 17, "the paramour of Antichrist."[23] The dualism of the true church and its false shadow proved a key component in the rise of Puritanism. Two theologians from Cambridge University, Thomas

Brightman (1562–1607) and Joseph Mede (1586–1639), proved highly influential in nurturing a Puritan millennialism that brought violent civil war in its wake.

Brightman's purpose, as the title of his book shows, *Revelation of Revelation . . . and Refutation of Robert Bellarmine* (1609), was to refute the interpretation of a Jesuit commentator named Robert Bellarmine. A brilliant controversialist, Bellarmine noted that the numerical values of the letters in Luther's name could be counted up to come to 666 (the number of the beast in Revelation 13:18), but that in reality the antichrist was neither Luther nor the papacy. Rather, the Revelation means to refer to a supernatural figure, rather than a present person or institution referred to symbolically.[24] Bellarmine and other Roman Catholic commentators came to this position not only to refute Protestants, but also to deal with followers of Joachim of Fiore within their ranks. In eschatological terms, the Counter-Reformation faced a theological war on two fronts: the Protestant attack on the institutional papacy as the antichrist, and the continued prophetic onslaught by followers of Joachim who invoked the authority of the Revelation against particular popes or papal policies. The response, enshrined in the Council of Trent, took Roman Catholic doctrine in a new, non-eschatological direction that identified the ultimate enemies of the church as supernatural and beyond historical identification.

To refute Catholic commentary on the Revelation, Brightman insisted, as Martin Luther had, that the events of the past had in fact fulfilled the prophecies of the text. To be sure, he identified events in his own English way, giving the English monarch a crucial role to play in the last days. Revelation 11:15 describes a pivotal moment in heaven coming to earth:

> The seventh angel trumpeted, and there were loud voices in heaven, saying, "The kingdom of the world has become the kingdom of our Lord and of his Messiah, and he will reign for ever and ever."

Brightman identified this text with Queen Elizabeth I's ascendancy to the throne, because she "gave her self and her kingdom to Christ by way of thankfulnesse, which she shewed: by rooting out the

Romish superstitions."[25] This permits him to interpret the seven vials of punishment in Revelation 16, culminating in Armageddon, as including the wrath unleashed against Rome by Queen Elizabeth. Yet after all, the defeat of the Spanish Armada could only have been accomplished by the inferior English force as the result of God's intervention.

To Brightman's mind, history had unfolded up until the time of the fourth vial of chapter 16: the campaign of Reformation still had much to accomplish. He forecast the fall of Rome in 1650. Yet his criticism of the Church of England as "luke-warm," in the manner of Laodicea in Revelation 3:14-21,[26] did not endear him to his country's establishment; his work saw publication only after his death (in 1607). He dated the thousand years of the saints' reign with the rise of forerunners of the Reformation such as John Wycliffe, the great translator of the New Testament and opponent of the papacy. Taking that as starting in 1300, that put the close of the millennium and the end of all things in 2300. Together with its dualistic reading of all church history in terms of the woman clothed with the sun in Revelation 12 and the whore of Babylon in Revelation 17, Puritan theology distinguished itself by a growing precision concerning the end times. Brightman advanced both those characteristics with effective exegesis of the Apocalypse.

English Reformer Joseph Mede's reading of the Revelation was more complex, more radical—and ultimately more influential—than Brightman's. Mede held that the text recapitulates the same events in three major sections (marked by Revelation 1:10, 4:10, and 10:8 respectively). Within this complexity, he also insisted, in a signal development of Puritan thought that contradicts Augustine's whole approach, that the millennium of Revelation 20 did *not* begin in the past, but awaits its dawn in the future:

> The seventh Trumpet, with the whole space of 1000 years thereto appertaining, signifying the great Day of Judgment, Circumscribed within two resurrections, beginning at the Judgment of Antichrist, as the morning of that day, and continuing during the space of 1000 years granted to new Jerusalem, (the Spouse of Christ) upon this Earth, till the universal resurrection and judgment of all the dead, when the wicked

> shall be cast into Hell to be tormented for ever, and the Saints translated into Heaven, to live with Christ for ever.[27]

With this exegesis, Mede returned to a pre-Augustinian understanding of where humanity stood in relation to the end of time. The precise correspondence posited between the Revelation's text and events on the earth made it clear to Mede that the millennium had not arrived after all, not even with the preaching of Wycliffe.

Mede's book was written against a background of current events that had the look of apocalypse, and apocalyptic motivations fed resort to violent action. Even as great religious wars were fought on the continent of Europe, Britain's dedication to accusing enemies of being the antichrist and claiming to be on the side of heaven, resulted in civil war and regicide. Brightman and Mede, for all their learning and their association with a preeminent university, gifted by royal endowments over the course of centuries, contributed to that outcome.

In almost every way a loyal Anglican, Mede undercut his chances of advancement in the Church of England by maintaining the radically antipapist rhetoric that Anglican leader William Laud (Archbishop of Canterbury) wanted to temper. But Mede's persistent identification of the papacy with the antichrist—and for good measure as the beasts of Revelation 13, and the false prophet of Revelation 16, as well as the whore of Revelation 17—assured him a favorable hearing among Puritans. John Milton and Isaac Newton, among many others, proved keen readers of Mede's *Clavis Apocalyptica* (*Key of the Revelation*, 1627).

Mede developed his work, not as a commentary, but as a critical approach to the text of the Apocalypse guided by its literary structure. He saw the resurrection of Revelation 20:5 and the millennium not as symbolic, but as genuine, a "proper and real" resurrection, as he said.[28] Because this was a divine act that intervened to change the conditions of the world and history definitively, Mede distanced himself from the traditional criticism of second-century millenarians, to the effect that they were materialist in their expectation. As a result he could claim the authority of Papias, Justin, Irenaeus, and Tertullian, without falling into what was perceived as their error.

Mede also defended his case by invoking rabbinic authority. Rabbi Qatina taught (*Sanhedrin* 97a) that the world endures seven thousand years, a conception embraced by David Kimhi, the medieval Jewish scholar whose work Mede consulted:

> Six thousand years shall the world exist, and one thousand shall it be desolate, as it is said (Isaiah 2:11), And the LORD shall be exalted in that day. . . . It has been said in accordance with Rabbi Qatina, just as the seventh year is one year of release in seven, so is the world, one thousand years out of seven shall be released.[29]

In detailing that approach in relation to the events of his time, Mede proved in Protestant circles to be as influential a force in the understanding of the Revelation as Joachim of Fiore had been in Roman Catholic circles. He gave the Puritans, and those who looked then—and those who look now—to the lead of a fully Protestant theology, a keen sense of the anticipation within human history of a fully supernatural millennium. Mede was not concerned with the moral millennium of Augustine, or with the spiritual *Status* of Joachim—his passion was the "proper and real" utopia that the final thousand years would bring.[30] In removing any suspicion of a materialist desire, he could focus with the intense Puritan passion to give God glory alone on the question of *when* the divine millennium would come.

As in the case of Joachim of Fiore, albeit in the interests of a different kind of millennium, Joseph Mede proceeded on the basis of a strict reading of the text. Once he saw the apocalyptic images as synchronic prophecies of the same events recapitulated in the three cycles within the Revelation, he let himself be guided by the wording of the Revelation to specify the times involved. The beast with ten horns in Revelation 17 must reign 1,260 years, the number corresponding to the prophecy of the two witnesses (Rev 11:3), the woman who flees (12:6) and the blasphemies of the beast (13:5)—all on the assumption that the reference to days stands for years. These indications lined up: the world still lived under the tyranny of the beast, and would do so for 1,260 years, until the millennium.

The crucial question naturally became: 1,260 years from what time in the past? Mede was emphatic that the cult of the saints, which he regarded as a form of idolatry, began during the fourth century, after the conversion of Constantine. In particular, Mede believed that the pope's idolatrous phase of reign began in 395 CE, so that 1655 would signal the end of the beast, and 1656 would mark the return of Christ. One of Mede's sympathizers, Archbishop James Ussher (who calculated the creation of the world to be 4004 BCE, and is cited by Creationists to this day), came up with a different set of dates—476 CE and 1736 CE, respectively. However calculated, Mede's rigorous reading implied that the millennium was coming soon, and his expectation and his method have found eager enthusiasts, detractors, and correctors.[31]

Mede published his *Clavis* in 1627 in Latin, followed by a commentary on the Revelation in 1632. Such was the influence of his work that the English Parliament (during its time as the reforming Long Parliament) endorsed its translation into English in 1643. From being a learned but largely marginal apocalyptic voice while he lived, in death Mede became the prophetic voice of Puritanism, endorsed by Parliament.

Mede's correlation between the Revelation and Daniel, in a synchronic reading of the dawn of the millennium, influenced in particular a group of radical reformers known as the Fifth Monarchy Men. They held that, after the four kingdoms enumerated by Daniel (chapter 7), a fifth kingdom corresponded to the millennium in Revelation. The end of the beast whose number was 666 was key to the dawn of this Fifth Monarchy, which they believed would occur in 1666 (1,000 years, plus 666 years). The beast concerned was not only the papacy but also the royal power in England that supported a system of bishops that was part of the beast's corruption. The Fifth Monarchy enthusiasts believed in the deposition of bishops, and ultimately of the king, with the force of apocalyptic mandate. William Aspinwall, who after twenty-two years in New England returned to England to join the cause, justified the beheading of Charles Stuart in 1649, by saying that "the saints' act of slaying the beast and taking away his dominion was no rash nor seditious act, but an act of sound judgment, approved by God."[32]

One of the Fifth Monarchist commissioners who signed the death warrant for Charles I, Thomas Harrison, was himself hung, drawn, and quartered in 1660, after the Restoration. He went to his fate with startling equanimity, according to a famous description by Samuel Pepys, who observed that it was his "chance to see the King beheaded at White Hall, and to see the first blood shed in revenge for the blood of the King at Charing Cross."[33] But that was not the end of the Fifth Monarchists. Thomas Venner—like Aspinwall, an arrival from Boston—led a revolt of Fifth Monarchists in London in 1661. He and several of his coleaders were also hung, drawn, and quartered. Even then, the lethal conflict between the divine right of kings and apocalyptic resistance to the beast had not ended, and the prospect of its resolution seemed dim indeed.

The Puritan revolution had turned readers of the Revelation into combatants. They knew that their enemies, whether papal or in the churches established by nation-states in Europe, were on the side of the antichrist in the very last phase of history. They understood that they, however, were literally on the side of the angels as God prepared his final, eschatological vindication of the just. War had become a duty, violence a virtue, suffering a necessity, and all because accomplished thinkers and writers such as Joseph Mede had integrated the Revelation within an apparently seamless intellectual vision that correlated history, divine intention and judgment, and insight into the future. Just as English academics, preeminently from Cambridge University, had pioneered this new prophetic vision with its galvanizing but also shattering force, so Cambridge in the next generation, in the contribution of its greatest scientist, would take the Puritan vision, refine its detail, refashion its content, and temper the white heat of Reformation with the discipline of analytic thought.

Further Reading

Bernard McGinn, *Antichrist: Two Thousand Years of the Human Fascination with Evil* (San Francisco: Harper, 1994); Robert E. Lerner,

"Ecstatic Dissent," *Speculum* 67, no. 1 (1992): 33–57; Gian Luca Potestà, "Radical Apocalyptic Movements in the Late Middle Ages," trans. Armando Maggi, in *Apocalypticism in Western History and Culture*, vol. 2, *The Encyclopedia of Apocalypticism*, ed. Bernard McGinn (New York: Continuum, 1999), 110–42; Irena Backus, *Reformation Readings of the Apocalypse: Geneva, Zurich, and Wittenberg*, Oxford Studies in Historical Theology (New York: Oxford University Press, 2000); Joseph Ratzinger, *The Theology of History in St. Bonaventure*, trans. Zachary Hayes (Chicago: Franciscan Herald Press, 1989); Heiko Oberman, "Teufelsdreck: Eschatology and Scatology in the 'Old' Luther," *The Sixteenth Century Journal* 19, no. 3 (1988): 435–50; and Crawford Gibbon, *The Puritan Millennium: Literature & Theology, 1550–1682* (Dublin: Four Courts, 2000), 42–43.

5

The Progress of the Saints

> And I saw a new heaven and a new earth, for the first heaven and the first earth had departed, and the sea is no longer. And I saw the Holy City, new Jerusalem, coming down out of heaven from God, prepared as a bride adorned for her husband. And I heard a loud voice from the throne saying, "Look, the dwelling of God is now with men, and he will dwell with them and they will be his peoples. And God himself will be with them and he will wipe away every tear from their eyes. And death will be no more, neither will there be mourning or crying or pain, for the first things have departed."
>
> Revelation 21:1-4

The year 1666 looked apocalyptic to many observers in England. Bubonic plague had by then established itself in London; during its course the epidemic killed between 15 and 20 percent of the city's population. In September, the Great Fire of London destroyed the urban center. Was all this connected to the beast whose number was 666 (Rev 13:18), added to the thousand years after Christ? In the millenarian environment that Puritan interpretation had established, one did not need to be a Fifth Monarchist to consider that possible.

The threat of plague made an undergraduate from Trinity College, Cambridge, return home. He studied mathematics during his retreat to his family's little manor house (at Woolsthorpe, near Grantham), and at the same time consulted his stepfather's theological library. His mentor at Cambridge, a professor and priest named Barrow, was a theologian as well as a mathematician. The combination did not seem unusual at the time.

The Scottish mathematician John Napier had already set the course for a synthesis of theology and mathematics at the end of the sixteenth century. Napier pioneered the use of logarithms and, in good Puritan fashion, he forecast the end of the papacy in 1688 or 1700 on the basis of his exegesis of the Revelation in his book, *A Plaine Discovery of the Whole Revelation* (1593). He offered a comprehensive and influential calendar of the end of days.

Napier determined that the seven seals of judgment in Revelation 6:1–8:1 each lasted seven years from the time of Christ. Taken together they climaxed in the destruction of the temple in 70 CE. Then came the seven trumpets of Revelation 8:2–11:19. Napier calculated that each of them covered 245 years, and the correspondence with dramatic events in history impressed him. He predicted the completion of the scheme in 1786, but later revised that estimate down to 1688 or 1700.[1] Here was exactly the sort of approach that Joseph Mede had mainstreamed within the University of Cambridge, but more finely tuned.

At home from Trinity, the refugee undergraduate read deeply in Puritan apocalypticism; inspired by Mede and Napier he set out to calculate the exact year of the coming of the millennium. The identification of the papacy with the beast and the whore of the Revelation were by then Puritan axioms, as was their persecution of the church for 1,260 days (Rev 12:6), taken as years. The crucial question remained, as it had for Mede, 1,260 years since what time? The interval between the emergence of the beast and the coming of the millennium was known; the unknown quantity was the date of the beast's emergence.

Because he never finalized his apocalyptic work for publication, the date that the precocious undergraduate came up with over the years for the defeat of the beast varied. He played with ranges of dates long after he became a professor at Cambridge and then left the university to become a government officer in

London. But he did come up with a more settled estimate toward the end of what proved a long life.

He wrote cautiously to an inquirer, dating events, like Napier, AC (for "After Christ," rather than AD, for *Anno Domini*, "Year of the Lord"):

> The period of 1260 days, if dated from the complete conquest of the three kings A.C. 800, will end A.C. 2060. It may end later, but I see no reason for its ending sooner.

The letter is written in the shakeir handwriting characteristic of its author in his later years. Having been knighted in 1705 for his scientific and professional service, he was responding to an inquiry to *Sir* Isaac Newton.

Isaac Newton's interest in the Revelation has perplexed many readers. Why would a scientist recognized as one of the princes of rationalism maunder in eschatological speculations? Attempts have been made to portray his apocalypticism as a marginal concern, or perhaps the product of his declining years and powers. These approaches run afoul of the persistent annotations and manuscripts produced over the entire course of Newton's exceptional career, including the periods when at Cambridge he developed the theories for which he is still renowned, and after he left for London in 1696 to head up the Royal Mint.

Segregating Newton's theological writings from his alchemical and scientific work, which remains common among historians of science, is symptomatic of the difficulty modern observers have often experienced in appreciating the range of his interests. Marginalizing Newton's apocalyptic investigations distorts our understanding of his basic orientation as a thinker. More crucially, misunderstanding Newton in this regard has fomented ignorance of a stream of interpretation of the Revelation that helped to shape the modern era.

In the field of physical science, Newton showed by inventing his calculus that gravity extends throughout the universe. That achievement, of course, required the support and research of other scientists (Galileo most of all). In the field of understanding the Revelation, as well, Newton proved a seminal figure. A Puritan by background, he shifted the entire emphasis of apocalyptic thinking from predictions of the future to a deep confidence in humanity under divine Providence.

Newton's famous theory of gravitation, which established his eminence after Edmund Halley coaxed him into writing *Naturalis Philosophiae Principia Mathematica*, did not pretend to offer a closed system of the universe. Newton believed, rather, that variations of observable phenomena implied divine action beyond the human capacity to understand. He elaborated an argument for God on the basis of his theory in his published "General Scholium" of 1713: "This most elegant system of the sun, planets, and comets could not have arisen without the design and dominion of an intelligent and powerful being."[2] In this domain, as in every field to which he turned his attention, Newton was committed to identifying underlying principles that ultimately derived from God.

When it came to biblical interpretation Newton was convinced that the Prophetic Books shared a mystical or allegorical language of symbols, both among themselves and with other cultures. As a result, prophecies could be related to specific events in retrospect by learning that language. His overall aim was not prediction, however, but the appreciation of the providential design of history. He wrote of previous approaches to the Revelation in a posthumously published commentary:

> The folly of Interpreters has been, to foretell times and things by this Prophecy, as if God designed to make them Prophets. By this rashness they have not only exposed themselves, but brought the Prophecy also into contempt. The design of God was much otherwise. He gave this and the Prophecies of the Old Testament, not to gratify mens curiosities by enabling them to foreknow things, but that after they were fulfilled they might be interpreted by the event, and his own Providence, not the Interpreters, be then manifested thereby to the world. For the event of things predicted many ages before, will then be a convincing argument that the world is governed by providence.[3]

This perspective marks a revolution in the approach to the Revelation, in its own way as dramatic and influential as Newton's theory of gravity. Newton cited Joseph Mede frequently and positively, pursuing his Puritan predecessor's means to a new end. Like Mede, he saw recapitulation operating within the text, so that different symbols appearing in different parts of the Revelation might refer to the same event. He also believed, as Mede did, that the coming millennium was supernatural; God would both raise the martyrs and give the living a place in the garden of paradise. Unlike Mede, however, Newton understood the point of the text not to be prediction at all, but the appreciation of divine purpose in history.

Nicholas of Lyra anticipated Newton's approach to the Revelation, in the same way that Galileo anticipated Newton's approach to gravity. In both cases Newton's genius was to seize on an organizing principle with unparalleled consistency, and to apply it more universally than had ever before been proposed.

In both science and theology Newton looked for the simplest, demonstrable cause of a given phenomenon, whether a fact of experience or a vision in the Apocalypse:

> As the world, which to the naked eye exhibits the greatest variety of objects, appears very simple in its internall constitution when surveyed by a philosophic understanding, & so much the simpler by how much the better it is understood, so it is in these visions. It is the perfection of God's works that they are all done with the greatest simplicity. He is the God of order & not of confusion. And therefore as they that would understand the frame of the world must indeavour to reduce their knowledg to all possible simplicity, so it must be in seeking to understand these visions.[4]

Hypotheses non fingo, Newton stated in the appended "General Scholium" to his *Principia,* "I do not devise hypotheses."[5] In reading the Revelation also, to posit a hypothetical Platonic world apart from the text, to which the text points as its real meaning, was—in his view—an unnatural adjustment. He therefore rejected Augustine's approach root and branch.

What was natural for Newton was to integrate the Revelation with precise and verifiable events of history. In fact, reading the Revelation and the book of Daniel together provided the key to his larger project of producing a complete global chronology. A person's mind should be able to view human history—that is, the past as interpreted by the two apocalyptic texts of Scripture, one from the Old Testament and one from the New Testament—with the same wonder, and the same mathematical precision, produced by considering how gravitation orders the natural macrocosm.

Notoriously secretive in much of his work, to the point of burning many manuscripts—probably alchemical—shortly before his death,[6] Newton published the scientific work for which he is best known after much prodding from supporters. His commentary on the Revelation only saw the light of day as a posthumous work, when his nephew had it printed. Yet during his lifetime he entered into correspondence concerning the text with Caroline (the Princess of Wales), discussing his chronology.

Newton pursued his innovative course at a time when the apocalyptic militancy that had fed the English Civil War was still in evidence. From his own entourage, a brilliant eccentric named Nicolas Fatio de Duillier joined the Camisards—self-declared prophets found guilty of terrorizing London after they predicted another great fire in 1707. His handpicked successor at Trinity College in Cambridge, William Whiston (the great translator of Josephus), continued Newton's chronological work, and reverted to Mede's style of predicting a swift end of the present age.

Newton offered no support of these views, but persisted in his providential historicism. He even saw a connection between the discovery of gravitation and the appreciation of divine purpose in history, which he called "alchemical history."[7] He could not predict a quickly arriving millennium, but its approach seemed palpable to him, in the dawn of new wisdom, both scientific and historical.

Newton's Progeny

Isaac Newton's triumph in his theory of gravitation was not by any stretch matched by fame as an interpreter of the Revelation. Voltaire famously remarked, "Sir Isaac Newton wrote his comment upon the Revelation to console mankind for the great superiority that he had over them in other respects."[8] After Newton's death, new attitudes prevailed in regard to the last book of the Bible and toward the universe, which made him seem prophetic in regard to science and backward in regard to the Revelation.

The universe was increasingly held to be a self-contained system, famously compared to a pocket watch by William Paley in 1802,[9] although that emphatically was not Newton's opinion. And according to a rising fashion, the Revelation had to do strictly with the past, rather than the lead up to the future. Even in Puritan theology anticipations of the end appeared discredited, and the view called "preterist," which sees the events in the Revelation as accomplished in the past, gained currency.

Newton's commentary was routinely dismissed, although it had been his contribution to insist that the accomplishment of the images could only be known *after the fact* even when they concerned the future. He was celebrated for a mechanical view of the universe and derided for a literal, futuristic view of apocalypse. Yet Newton espoused neither of those views. The Enlightenment remade one of its founders in its own image, by revering a science Newton did not propose and rejecting a form of prophecy far less sophisticated than his recourse to Providence.

The preterist perspective reads the Revelation exclusively with reference to events in the past. The past in question might be the past of John of Patmos or the past of his readers; in either case, the point is that the book refers to events that have already happened. As this point of view gathered adherents, Newton's orientation lost credibility, even with his caution against the "folly" of pretending "to foretell times and things by this Prophecy."[10] Newton believed that we could only know the meaning of images when they had been fulfilled, although they pointed to the future. Preterists maintained that the images had already found their references.

A concurrent perspective often associated with preterism maintains that Christ's return is actually only to occur after the millennium, since that second coming is obviously not in the past of John of Patmos or of any of his readers. Any events referred to in the text do not include Christ's definitive advent to rule the world. For this reason, the perspective is called "post-millennial," as compared to the "pre-millennial" views of Mede and those who thought along his lines.[11]

Until that post-millennial moment, signs of the approaching consummation must take the form of the increasing acceptance of the preaching of Christ, as a result of Satan's binding in Revelation 20:2. That implies, as the Revelation specifies, that the saints will "reign with Christ" (20:4), without saying that Jesus returns to earth when they do. He is enthroned in heaven; they rule on an earth protected from Satan's deceit. The progress of the saints marked the nearest that humanity could come to the final consummation, giving the progressive view of history a new and fatefully important impetus.

This picture of an advance toward the consummation was pursued by an eighteenth century Connecticut pastor who became America's foremost theologian of that period (and some scholars would say, of any period). Jonathan Edwards (1703–1758) exemplified a political as well as religious consciousness of progress that remains influential to this day:

> God is continually causing revolutions. Providence makes a continual progress, and continually is bringing forth things new in the state of the world, and very different from what ever were before. He removes one that He may establish another. And perfection will not be obtained till the last revolution, when God's design will be fully reached.[12]

Jonathan Edwards could no more resist speculating on when the papal antichrist would fall than Newton could. He wrote privately that the event might come in 1866—as it turned out a little over a century after his own death.

But this sort of prediction was out of character for Edwards. There is a clear line of restraint linking the mature Edwards and the mature Newton; they both stopped short of programmatic prediction, and of public apocalyptic forecasts, even as they maintained a progressive view of the future.

The distinctive power of Edwards' perspective did not reside in prediction, nor even in his stress on Providence, although Edwards shared that with Newton. Edwards' experience convinced him that humanity's awareness of Christ's redemption was growing, and that the revival of that awareness featured as part of God's plan of salvation. Revival occurs incrementally, beginning in the first century: "the light of the gospel, which first began to dawn and glimmer immediately after the fall, gradually increases the nearer we come to Christ's time." Thereafter, "Christ's coming in his kingdom" proceeds in four stages: the resurrection is succeeded by the accession of Constantine (which Edwards assessed positively, unlike Newton), the overthrow of the antichrist (in the form of the papacy), and the last judgment.[13]

At each stage, the advance is preceded by darkness, which Edwards acknowledged complicates any attempt at forecast, saying, "Whether the times shall be any darker still, or how much darker before the beginning of this glorious work of God, we can't tell."[14] Yet the fact of revival remained for Edwards incontrovertible, as demonstrated by this passage from *Some Thoughts Concerning the Present Revival of Religion in New England* (1743):

> 'Tis not unlikely that this work of God's Spirit, that is so extraordinary and wonderful, is the dawning, or at least the prelude, of that glorious work of God, so often foretold in Scripture, which in the progress and issue of it, shall renew the world of mankind. If we consider how long since the things foretold, as what should precede this great event, have been accomplished, and how long this event has been expected by the church of God, and thought to be nigh by the most eminent men of God in the church; and withal consider what the state of things now is, and has for a considerable time been, in the church of God and world of mankind, we can't reasonably think otherwise, than that the beginning of this great work of God must be near. And there are many things that make it probable this work will begin in America.[15]

Edwards' view forged a link between progress toward the millennium and the revival of Christ in human awareness, so that *the experience of God in itself became a sign of redemption.* In particular, the thought that revival in America had special significance had been sown, and would prove a hardy perennial in American religious rhetoric both before and after the armed revolution that produced the United States.

As in the case of most approaches to reading the Revelation, Edwards' built upon earlier views, but his theology of the significance of revival provided his perspective with fresh, coordinating force. The importance of revival also led Edwards to see signs of the millennium less in external events than in a renewed commitment to Christ. Consequently, he avoided the rigid distinction within Protestant theology between those who saw Christ coming before the millennium, and those who saw the millennium as an event before Christ's coming. He dialed back the dispute between "pre-millennialists" and "post-millennialists," because in his analysis the millennium was identified precisely with the revived awareness of Christ.

Edwards did not equate Christ with Jesus as a historical figure, but saw Jesus as the fulcrum balancing the whole history of redemption that realized Christ. Where for Newton the near vacuum of the universe was filled with Christ, for Edwards knowing Christ brought one to a millennial recognition. His apocalyptic analysis went hand in hand with his philosophy of nature, in which, he said, "those beings which have knowledge and consciousness are the only proper and real and substantial beings . . . [hence] spirits only are properly substance."[16] He says in almost Newtonian prose, "The works of God are but a kind of voice or language of God, to instruct intelligent beings in things pertaining to himself."[17]

Edwards took a commonly accepted view of Providence and applied it to understanding the millennium, much as Newton had. He then translated the awareness of Providence into religious revival. When he speaks of "consciousness" it is in the meaning of cognition of God as well as of oneself in terms of truly spiritual being.

Progressive Millennium

William Blake (1757–1817), the Romantic poet and painter born a year before Edwards' death, pursued a commitment more radical than Edwards' to the significance of consciousness as connection to God. Blake's contribution was to develop an experiential reading of the Revelation, according to which its truth is realized by and within the human mind, not along the scale of history.

Blake's great innovation was to see time, not as a calculation by the exterior measurement of elapsed intervals, but rather as a guide to the nature of interior experience. In his time-dissolving scheme, the only intervals that matter are inside the mind itself.

In his epic *Milton*, Blake related the classic scheme of seven thousand-year periods to the inner, indeed biological, recognition of which humans are capable:

> Every Time less than a pulsation of the artery
> Is equal in its period & value to Six Thousand Years.[18]

Blake immediately prefaces this time-dissolving assertion with a chronological analysis that focuses on the interval of two hundred years,[19] the time since the birth of John Milton:

> Now Seven Ages is amounting to Two Hundred Years
> Each has its Guard. Each Moment Minute Day Month &
> Year.
> All are the work of Fairy hands of the Four Elements
> The Guard are Angels of Providence on duty evermore.[20]

Because poetry captures the "pulsation of an artery," it gathers revelatory force as the corpus of the work extends.

Blake's insight took him to a place where Edwards did not travel: to a place where the fact of eternity reconfigured the reality of time so that it became, not a calendar at all, but a map toward elevated awareness. He saw the significance of "six thousand years," as pointing to the seventh and last millennium, but saw the possibility of realizing that moment within a heartbeat.

As in the case of Edwards and Newton, Blake posited his apprehension of God in relation to a view of natural philosophy. He did so more succinctly than Edwards, and with greater confidence in how God may be known. In "All Religions Are One," Blake offered a powerful analogy, "As the true method of knowledge is experiment the true faculty of knowing must be the faculty which experiences."[21]

"Knowledge" here refers to what is known, while "knowing" means the process by which knowledge is accomplished. Although categorized as a Romantic poet, and famously opposed to the mechanical application of Newton's science to understand the world and human experience, Blake was also capable of a syllogistic defense of his insights. "All Religions Are One" sets out a series of interlocking assertions. His statement about knowledge and knowing is "the Argument" that is followed by seven principles intended to show that man as "Poetic Genius" is the source of knowing and for that reason of the unity of religions.

Blake is clear that this "knowing" represents, not only the principal occupation of humanity, but also the true substance of being, as he announced in *Jerusalem*, a poem that looks forward to the heavenly city of the Revelation built "in England's green and pleasant land."[22] He conceives of this knowledge in terms of scriptural allusions to the principles of faith (some of which are identified here within square brackets):

> I know of no other Christianity and of no other Gospel than the liberty both of body & mind to exercise the Divine Arts of Imagination.
>
> Imagination the real & eternal World of which this Vegetable Universe is but a faint shadow & in which we shall live in our Eternal or Imaginative Bodies, when these Vegetable Mortal Bodies are no more [1 Cor 15:35-55]. The Apostles knew of no other Gospel. What were all their spiritual gifts [1 Cor 12]? What is the Divine Spirit? is the Holy Ghost any other than an Intellectual Fountain? What is the Harvest of the Gospel & its Labours [Luke 10:2; John 4:35; Rev 14:15]? What is that Talent which it is a curse to hide [Matt 25:14-30]? Where are the Treasures of Heaven which we are to lay for ourselves, are they any other than Mental Studies & Performances [Matt 6:19-21; Luke 12:33-34]? What are all the Gifts of the Gospel, are they not all Mental Gifts? Is God a Spirit who must be worshipped in Spirit & in Truth and are not the Gifts of the Spirit Every-thing to Man?[23]

In his insistence on the divine property of humanity itself, Blake dedicates himself to a reading of the Scriptures that understands with St. Paul, "Now is acceptable time; now is salvation's day" (2 Cor 6:2).

Blake's conviction of the fierce importance of the moment involved an urgent reading of the Revelation. Writing in *Milton*, he said he believed he could identify the two witnesses of Revelation, chapter 11, as preachers of his own time—George Whitfield and John Wesley (mangling the spelling of their names in doing so):

> He sent his two Servants Whitefield & Westley; were they
> Prophets

Or were they Idiots or Madmen? Shew us Miracles!
Can you have greater Miracles than these? Men who devote
Their lifes whole comfort to entire scorn & injury & death.[24]

George Whitfield, whose collaboration was dear to Edwards, and John Wesley (in some ways the English counterpart of Edwards) here appear as harbingers of precisely the self-consciousness that Blake identified with the millennium.

Not inclined to content himself with the mere signs of the millennium such as Edwards had looked for, Blake's passionate focus was the substance of the millennium, which he saw realized in the human mind. In his epic poem *The Four Zoas* he uses the imagery of the marriage of the Lamb from Revelation 19, the heavenly Jerusalem (Rev 21), and the woman who gives birth (Rev 12) in order to articulate his vision of a new humanity:

Thus shall the male & female live in the life of Eternity
Because the Lamb of God Creates himself a bride & wife
That we his Children evermore may live in Jerusalem
Which now descendeth out of heaven a City yet a Woman
Mother of myriads redeemd & born in her spiritual palaces
By a New Spiritual birth Regenerated from Death.[25]

This Jerusalem can indeed be planted on England's green and pleasant land,[26] because "the stones are pity, and the bricks, well wrought affections: / Enameld with love & kindness."[27]

This is the basis on which Blake can exhort each Christian to "engage himself openly & publicly before all the World in some Mental pursuit for the Building up of Jerusalem."[28] But in the end there is no easy optimism for a poet who had seen the promise of the French Revolution dissolve into savagery. In particular, he came to see the Enlightenment culture of rational deism as itself the synagogue of Satan of which Revelation spoke (2:9, 3:9), and he looked upon it with the same disdain his predecessors had reserved for the papacy, comparing it to Babylon.

In *Jerusalem* he portrayed the deists as enemies opposed to Christianity, but also as threatening humanity because they reduced "Man" to his "Vegetated Spectre": "Man must & will have Some Religion; if he has not the Religion of Jesus, he . . . will erect the Synagogue of Satan calling the Prince of this World,

God; and destroying all who do not worship Satan under the Name of God."[29] This is the basis on which he can launch into a prophetic attack:

> When Satan first the black bow bent
> And the Moral Law from the Gospel rent
> He forged the Law into a Sword
> And spilld the blood of mercys Lord.
> Titus! Constantine, Charlemain!
> O Voltaire! Rousseau! Gibbon Vain
> Your Grecian Mocks & Roman Sword
> Against this image of his Lord!
> For a Tear is an Intellectual thing;
> And a Sigh is the Sword of an Angel King
> And the bitter groan of a Martyrs woe
> Is an Arrow from the Almighties Bow![30]

The close of Blake's *Europe*, with its violent imagery of judgment against empire, has been compared to "the avenging Christ of Saint John's prediction" (in Rev 19:11-15).[31] Blake's recourse to the Revelation, to confront authority by absorbing apocalyptic language within his own poetry, recalls Thomas Müntzer's, and reflects the continuing millennialism of his own time typified by Immanuel Swedenborg.[32] Swedenborg developed a theory of Christ's invisible second coming in 1757, so that his biblical calendar could be seen as vindicated by the elect few who could perceive this spiritual event.

Even folded within Blake's self-presentation as a prophet, the text of the Revelation shines through. In addition to the unmistakable references to Babylon and the synagogue of Satan, in *Milton* Blake compares the printing press to the winepress of war, an inverted image, since this press is not God's (as in Rev 14:17-20), but "before the Seat / Of Satan," itself a reference to the Revelation's reference to Satan's throne in Pergamum (Rev 2:13).[33] When he referred to the contents of the Bible as "builded with immortal labour" by the "Divine Lord," he mentioned only "the Four-fold Gospel, and the Revelations everlasting."[34] That allusion to Revelation 14:6 makes the last book of the New Testament its own "eternal gospel," and casts one of Blake's last major works, *The Everlasting Gospel*, as a poetic and ethical apocalypse.[35]

On the other side of the Atlantic from Blake, a decidedly nonliterary but influential reading of the Revelation also arose from a visionary quarter. John Woolman (1720–1772) was an American Quaker of modest means and education whose visions—which he usually referred to as "openings"—fed a nascent antislavery movement that only became politically consequential more than half of a century after his death. Woolman recorded his openings from very early in his life, as a schoolboy.[36] He refers in the initial entry in his *Journal* to some teasing from his companions, and his withdrawal from them to read Revelation 22, where the text refers to a river of the water of life issuing from the throne of God and from Christ as the Lamb of God. "In reading it," wrote Woolman:

> my mind was drawn to seek after and long for that pure habitation which I then believed God had prepared for his servants. The place where I sat and the sweetness that attended my mind remains fresh in my memory.[37]

In a manner that recalls Blake, although with an entirely different sensibility, Woolman kept his attention focused on a glory that could not be taken away. That focus saw him through situations that would have brought lesser minds to despair.

While he worked for a shopkeeper in his native Mount Holly, New Jersey, Woolman's employer asked him to write a bill of sale for a black woman. He wrote, "The thoughts of writing an instrument of slavery for one of my fellow creatures felt uneasy."[38] That unease, a product of the integrity of Woolman's soul, propelled him to oppose slavery. His abolitionist philosophy, which he articulated most fully in his *Some Considerations on the Keeping of Negroes* in 1754, became part and parcel of who he was.

Woolman's attention to what was present or what was stirring in his mind forms a thread that runs throughout his life and thought. Ralph Waldo Emerson spoke of Woolman as offering a practical philosophy and a clear insight, which Emerson compared with that of the New Testament.[39] The focus of Woolman's insight, as reflected in his journal, was frequently the Revelation of John, although he did not burden his writing with citations. Referring to the early part of his life, Woolman described how he managed to throw off some tendencies toward dissolution:

> As I lived under the cross, and simply followed the opening of truth, my mind, from day to day, was more enlightened, my former acquaintance were left to judge of me as they would, for I found it safest for me to live in private, and keep these things sealed up in my own breast.
>
> While I silently ponder on that change wrought in me, I find no language equal to convey to another a clear idea of it. I looked upon the works of God in this visible creation, and an awfulness covered me; my heart was tender and often contrite, and universal love to my fellow-creatures increased in me. This will be understood by such as have trodden in the same path. Some glances of real beauty may be seen in their faces who dwell in true meekness. There is a harmony in the sound of that voice to which divine love gives utterance, and some appearance of right order in their temper and conduct whose passions are regulated. Yet all these do not fully show forth that inward life to those who have not felt it, but this white stone and new name is only known rightly by such as receive it.[40]

The "white stone" at the close of this reflection alludes to Revelation 2:17: "Whoever has ears, hear what the Spirit says to the churches. To the one who is victorious, I will give him of the hidden manna, and I will give him a white stone, and upon the stone a new name written, which no one knows except the one who receives it." Woolman—like Blake, but with complete independence—read the Revelation as a map of the experience of God, and acknowledged its power to promote social change.

Woolman's combination of social conscience and existential confidence proved to be a potent mix that fueled great efforts at social reform in the nineteenth century, including abolitionism, the prohibition of child labor, demands for suitable working conditions and hours, and public support for the disadvantaged and impoverished. The Civil War, the introduction of progressive legislation, and governmental efforts at controlling monopolistic abuses all provided impetus to this dual emphasis on change and confidence.

The piety of this movement, which peaked in what came to be known as the Social Gospel, can be gauged by a poem written by the American theologian and Baptist minister Walter Rauschenbusch (1861–1918) as he lay dying:

In the castle of my soul
Is a little postern gate,
Whereat, when I enter,
I am in the presence of God.
In a moment, in the turning of a thought,
I am where God is.
This is a fact.[41]

The sense of a timeless union with God, an inheritance from Blake, influenced not only Rauschenbusch, but also the movement known as "theosophy," an attempt (dating from the time of the Reformation) to discover divine wisdom across the barriers of different religions and understandings of science and philosophy. One of the most important of theosophical teachers was Helena Petrovna Blavatsky (1831–1891), who developed an explicitly allegorical interpretation, for example in her exegesis of Revelation 16:8-9, where the fourth angel pours his vial on the sun, and is given power to scorch humanity. She sees this as when "every soul becomes purified of its sins, and unites itself forever with its spirit," and claims the passage as support for a heliocentric cosmology.[42] Although philosophically more systematic than Blake, and more reflective than Rauschenbusch, Blavatsky captured the sense of the Revelation as an eternal message.

Helena Blavatsky's contemporary, Christina Rossetti, spent the last years of her life writing a devotional commentary on the Apocalypse, in which the images are explored liturgically as well as in literary terms. The "woman clothed with the sun" in Revelation 12:1, for example, encapsulates Eve, the Virgin Mary, Mary Magdalene, and the church all at once. That compounding of images is reminiscent of the visions of Hildegard of Bingen, and the meaning Rossetti saw here echoes the medieval writers she had studied, "As love of his Lord enabled St. Peter to tread the sea, so love of the same Lord sets weak woman immovable on the waves of this troublesome world."[43]

Rauschenbusch's emphasis was far more activist. To him progress grounded in God appeared irresistible, and an outgrowth of the Reformation. According to this mindset, progress is as relentlessly inevitable as the Revelation itself and Newton's principles:

> The modern emancipation of the intellectual life began in the Renaissance of the fifteenth century and is not finished yet. The modern emancipation of the religious life began in the Reformation of the sixteenth century and is not finished yet. The modern emancipation of the political life began in the Puritan revolution of the seventeenth century and is not finished yet. The modern emancipation of the industrial life began in the nineteenth century and is not finished yet. Let us have patience. Let us have hope. And above all let us have faith.[44]

In particular, Rauschenbusch believed that "the millennial hope is the social hope of Christianity," consisting of "a perfect social life, victory over all the evil that wounds and mars human intercourse and satisfaction for the hunger and thirst after justice, equality, and love."[45] This, the kingdom of God, was the communal counterpart of eternal life for the individual, and together they made up "a perfect religious hope." Apocalyptic literature could express this hope, even under paralyzing conditions of oppression.

Rauschenbusch expressed optimism at the close of his most famous book in the manner of other early twentieth-century reformers impressed with dramatic improvements in material conditions. Even the clouds of war, and then the reality of carnage on a global scale, did not diminish his faith; his confidence in progress did not fade, nor did he desist from an American exceptionalism reminiscent of Jonathan Edwards' evocation of America as a shining city on a hill.[46] But then it turned out that the most negligible of concerns—an issue connected directly with the Revelation of John—would subvert confidence in the Social Gospel, and see its eclipse within the twentieth century by the rise of a new apocalyptic understanding.

Further Reading

The principal thinkers discussed in this chapter have been analyzed extensively. See Frank E. Manuel, *The Religion of Isaac Newton: The Freemantle Lectures 1973* (Oxford: Clarendon, 1974), 83–104; Stephen D. Snobelen, "'God of Gods, and Lord of Lords': The Theology of Isaac Newton's General Scholium to the *Principia*," *Osiris* 16 (2001): 169–208; the electronic resource in "The Newton

Project," available at http://www.newtonproject.sussex.ac.uk/prism.php?id=44; Avihu Zakai, *Jonathan Edwards's Philosophy of Nature: The Re-enchantment of the World in the Age of Scientific Reasoning* (London: T&T Clark, 2010); Harold Fisch, *The Biblical Presence in Shakespeare, Milton, and Blake: A Comparative Study* (Oxford: Clarendon, 1999), 262–63; Robert Rix, *William Blake and the Cultures of Radical Christianity* (Aldershot: Ashgate, 2007); E. P. Thompson, *Witness Against the Beast: William Blake and the Moral Law* (Cambridge: Cambridge University Press, 1993); and Donovan E. Smucker, *The Origins of Walter Rauschenbusch's Social Ethics* (Montreal: McGill-Queen's University Press, 1994).

6

Hell on Earth

> After this I saw another angel coming down from heaven, having great authority, and the earth was illuminated by his glory. And he shouted with a strong voice, saying: Fallen! Fallen is Babylon the Great! And she has become a dwelling for demons and a haunt for every unclean spirit, a haunt for every unclean bird, a haunt for every unclean and detested beast. For from the wine of the wrath of her fornication all the nations have fallen. The kings of the earth fornicated with her, and the merchants of the earth grew rich from the force of her indulgences.
>
> Revelation 18:1-3

Jonathan Edwards encouraged the progressive view of the millennium that saw its dawning in contemporary religious experience, rather than requiring the arrival of Christ in his second coming. But Joseph Mede's insistence that Revelation 20:5 promises the *parousia* with a "real and proper" resurrection had by no means been forgotten. Eventually, it bubbled up amidst the movements of religious revival during the early nineteenth century known as the Second Great Awakening, and transformed the way many Americans conceived of the Apocalypse. That new American conception—as we will see—reshaped Judaism and Islam, as well as Christianity, during the twentieth century.

Within the Puritan understanding of the millennium championed by Joseph Mede, the Revelation became the lens through which other Scriptures were read. In this way, St. Paul's reference to how believers would meet with Christ in his second coming was spliced into the description of the moment of resurrection in Revelation 20:5. Paul speaks of living believers who have survived those who have already died, and promises that they will be united to meet Jesus as their Lord:

> This we say by a word of the Lord, that we who are alive, remaining until the *parousia* of the Lord will not precede those who have slept. Because the Lord himself by a command, with the sound of an archangel and with God's trumpet, will descend from heaven, and the dead in Christ will arise first, then we who are alive, remaining, will be snatched up together with them in clouds to meet the Lord in the air, and so will we always be with the Lord. So reassure one another with these words. (1 Thess 4:15-18)

Puritan circles conceived of the "rapture" (as the reference in 1 Thessalonians came to be called), the millennium of the Apocalypse, and the second coming of Christ as all combined in a single moment of divine judgment.

Such was the case in the writings of the New England Puritan ministers Increase Mather (1639–1723) and his son Cotton Mather (1663–1728); they portrayed the saints as being taken up into the air in order to avoid the carnage left behind on the earth. Those "left behind" after the rapture faced hell on earth, a scenario that came to be reinforced over time. This became the classic pre-millenarian view, according to which Christ's second coming needed to happen before the millennium could begin. It contrasted to the post-millenarian perspective that Rauschenbusch developed—with its emphasis on the progress through the millennium until the second coming—under the influence of thinkers such as Isaac Newton, Jonathan Edwards, John Woolman, and William Blake.

Pre-millenarian views in America surged in popularity during the nineteenth century in a series of religious revival movements, each associated with a fresh wave of apocalyptic forecasts. The most famous movement centered on Baptist preacher William Miller. Miller's appeal was widespread; part of his attraction lay in a growing impatience with academic authority in the reading of Scripture, and opposition to hierarchy in the life of faith. At the same time, he pursued a passionate interest in the rational understanding of biblical chronology.

Miller's life encapsulates the conditions that favored the emergence of a new pre-millennialism as a result of disappointment in the optimism of a progressive approach to the promise of Revelation 20. After the war of 1812, in which Miller served, and the deep financial crisis that culminated in the panic of 1837, hope in gradual progress toward prophetic fulfillment no longer appeared plausible. Miller's increasingly intense engagement with the Scriptures convinced him of Jesus' personal concern for believers, and of his imminent, supernatural intervention on their behalf. When he published a collection of the biblical passages that most inspired him, he relied repeatedly on the "rapture" passage from 1 Thessalonians, as well as on Revelation 20—read together as describing the same event.[1]

The millennium also promised a new Jerusalem in a new heaven and a new earth, and Miller put out a pamphlet in 1844 that set out the full sequence of events, beginning with the rapture, which was to occur on a precise date: October 22, 1844.[2] He saw the rapture as fulfilling Jesus' parable in Matthew 25:1-13 of the bridegroom coming at midnight and finding wise virgins ready with oil lamps to meet him for the wedding feast, while foolish virgins missed the feast because of their lack of preparation. So Miller declared "the midnight cry," although the details of timing could not be derived from that parable. But because he saw that wedding feast in Matthew in terms of the Wedding of the Lamb in Revelation 19:6-10, he had a ready resource to determine the timing of the midnight cry: the Apocalypse of John.

Miller based his forecast on the understanding that the Apocalypse involves recapitulations. Revelation 14 therefore marks the judgment of Jesus from Mount Zion as both the Lamb of God and the Son of Man *at the outset of the seventh millennium* as described in Revelation 20. Believing also that the Apocalypse and Daniel shared a common calendar, he deduced that the reference in Daniel 8:14 to the cleansing of the temple after 2,300 days really referred to years. He timed the outset of John's millennium from an edict of Artaxerxes to rebuild the temple in 487 BCE, yielding Miller's date in 1844, allowing for intercalations in the Jewish calendar.

The disappointment resulting from the failure of his forecast was bitter, especially to those who had given their property away in advance of the date and found they had no legal recourse for getting it back. But Miller's approach continued in the view of Seventh-Day Adventists, who taught that the temple Jesus cleansed was in heaven, rather than on the earth. One of Miller's followers, named Hiram Edson, described a vision that gave new meaning to the parable of the wedding feast and to the temple:

> Instead of our High Priest coming out of the Most Holy of the heavenly sanctuary to come to this earth on the tenth day of the seventh month, at the end of the 2,300 days, he for the first time entered on that day the second apartment of the sanctuary; and that he had a work to perform in the most holy before coming to this earth. That he came to the marriage at that time; in other words, to the Ancient of days to receive kingdom, dominion, and glory; and we must wait for his return *from the wedding.*[3]

Pre-millennial expectation could be preserved without denying the authenticity of William Miller's teaching, by shifting the prophecy's target from earth to heaven. What Mede called the "real and proper" resurrection could still be anticipated, without insisting upon its timing in earthly terms. A similar adjustment, to speak of Christ's coming in a way not fully recognized, was introduced by Charles Taze Russell into the teaching of the group that came to be known as the Jehovah's Witnesses.[4] He taught that Christ had returned invisibly in 1874, and that 1914 signaled a transition into the millennium.

The Anglo-Irish priest John Nelson Darby (1800–1882) also pursued a pre-millenarian reading of 1 Thessalonians 4:17 within an apocalyptic scenario inspired by the Revelation. Unlike William Miller he did so without specifying a date. In the 1830s he developed his teaching of the rapture as an instantaneous but unpredictable event. Relying heavily on the "rapture" passage (1 Thess 4:17) and its pairing with the book of Revelation, Darby added an innovation: the prediction of seven years of tribulation at the hands of the antichrist for those who remained on earth. They run the gauntlet of tribulation, and are subjected to the thousand-year rule of the saints after the Armageddon of Revelation 16:16. All that is only preliminary to final judgment. This comprehensive expectation, and its avoidance of Miller's precise prediction, made Darby's views attractive in America both during his life and long after.

Walter Rauschenbusch attempted to dismiss expectation of the rapture as "faith in catastrophes,"[5] but it had emerged in Darby's perspective as the necessary response, guided by God's justice, to the injustice of this world. Only an abrupt shift in the ages could bring the dawn of Christ's kingdom. Darby's single-mindedness and dedicated preaching far and wide led to the rapid spread of this pre-millenarian religious yearning. His theology of "dispensations," successive epochs of God's relationship to humanity, became widespread.[6] They included the seven generations of Adam, Noah, Abraham, Israel, the Gentiles, the church, and—finally—the millennium, the last initiated by the rapture and completing the sequence of seven established in the Apocalypse. The content of the dispensations derives from the Bible as a whole, but their number and the means by which one leads to another were spelled out, in Darby's view,[7] in the Revelation of John.

Darby predated the emergence of twentieth-century Fundamentalism, but the rise of the modern Fundamentalist movement provided a boost to his theology. He read the Bible—as later Fundamentalists wished to—as an inerrant whole. Putting 1 Thessalonians and the Revelation together was from this point of view not an anachronism, but a faithful assertion that the Scripture forms a seamless whole.

A single publication supported both Dispensationalism and Fundamentalism during their extraordinary advance in America during the twentieth century. In 1909 Cyrus Scofield first published his *Reference Bible* with Oxford University Press; the book consisted of the King James Version with Dispensationalist notes, and eventually a chronology that included Archbishop Ussher's dating of creation to 4004 BCE. Presented as part of an already widely cherished translation of the Bible, Dispensationalism and Fundamentalism both appeared to be traditional forms of Christianity.

Seismic events in the history of the twentieth century favored the rise of Dispensationalist Fundamentalism. World War I gave the lie to the idea of the steady progress of Western civilization, and particularly to idealistic views of the efficacy of government. And how could you deride "faith in catastrophes," when catastrophic events, quickly and fully reported by an unprecedented increase of mass communication from the turn of the last century onward, became routine news in the experience of virtually everyone in the developed world?

Scofield scoffed at the idea of any form of progressive evolution. He so abhorred the myth of progress that he even held—detailing his comment in exposition on 2 Thessalonians 2:3—that "the predicted future of the visible church is apostasy."[8] People in themselves are not perfectible, and their attempts at perfection bring only corruption. Most Christians would be left behind while only true believers were raptured. When leaders such as Rauschenbusch criticized his theology or his personal life, Scofield portrayed them to be agents of Satan "transformed as the ministers of righteousness."[9]

Aimee Semple McPherson, the Pentecostal revivalist whose ministry from her Angelus Temple in Los Angeles pioneered evangelical Christianity as a media phenomenon, developed a more optimistic strain of apocalyptic expectation. Founded in 1923, her Temple hosted anti-evolution Fundamentalists such as William Jennings Bryan and embraced a pre-millennialist position, according to which the Pentecostal movement itself was "God's final instrument in the 'last days' to restore his church before Armageddon."[10]

In her presentation of herself, McPherson was also such an instrument. She produced a monthly magazine, the *Bridal Call*, and explained that imagery as a combination of just such texts that William Miller had relied on, the parable of the virgins from Matthew's Gospel (25:1-13), the Wedding of the Lamb in the Revelation (19:6-10), and the new Jerusalem adorned as a bride in the Revelation (21:2). She called her female followers to take on the "*white robes*" of Christ's righteousness—an image that invokes Revelation (6:11; 7:9, 13-14), and literally garbed herself in white during her trademark "illustrated sermons."[11]

McPherson described the actual meeting of the bride of Christ and her spouse as "that meeting in the air" in a sermon called "The Marriage of the Lamb":

> At last He clasps her in His arms; she for whom He died, and has waited so long. At last she lays her queenly head upon the bosom of Him for whom she lived, and has pictured so often in her dreams. He wipes away her tears. Their lips meet as they embrace.[12]

She developed this encounter out of the text she cites in the King James Version, from Revelation 19:7: "Let us be glad and rejoice, and give honor to Him, for the marriage of the Lamb hath come, and the wife hath made herself ready." In addition, of course, the "meeting in the air" draws on William Miller's marriage of the scene in Revelation with 1 Thessalonians 4:17. McPherson's interpretation drew fire for its sensuality, but perhaps its greater power lies in its contradiction of the encyclical of Pope Pius X in 1904 (*Ad Diem Illum Laetissimum*) which, in the tradition of Hildegard of Bingen and Christina Rossetti, identified the woman clothed with the sun in Revelation 12:1 with the Virgin Mary, understood as the Immaculate Conception (that is, her being conceived without sin). To McPherson, the woman of the Apocalypse was rather the emergent church of her time.

In her mind, this Pentecostal rebirth of Spirit, the last phase before the millennium, demonstrated believers' purity in trenchant opposition to communism. She vigorously applied herself to anticommunism in the last phase of her life (before her death from an overdose of sedatives in 1944), following the lead of pre-millennialist teachers who preceded her. Within the tradition of pre-millennialist prophecy during the nineteenth century, Scofield had predicted the Jews' return to Palestine, and portrayed the apocalyptic "Gog" (Rev 20:8) as Russia. At the dawn of the twentieth century, these seemed distant events to most observers, and improbable to many.

But then came the aftermath of the twentieth century's second calamitous World War, with the establishment of the State of Israel in 1948 and the start of the Cold War—in which the Soviet Union emerged as the major antagonist of the United States. These events became irresistible signs for some of God's impending and definitive intervention in the rapture, the tribulation, and the millennium. The stage was set for a new dispensation and a fusing of Christian Fundamentalism with American patriotism.

Books such as Hal Lindsey's *The Late, Great Planet Earth*[13] encouraged the expectation of an imminent pre-millennial return of Christ and the start of a new millennium very, very soon. The calendars and exact predictions varied, of course, from writer to writer, but their specificity meant that Darby's reticence about calculating the time of the end was definitively left behind, as in this forecast:

> By the fall of 2008, the United States will have collapsed as a world power, or it will have begun its collapse and no longer exist as an independent nation within six months after that time. There is a marginal, six-month window of time that God has not yet revealed concerning this specific moment of time. This will be revealed some time soon after the distribution of this book begins.[14]

The welter of competing apocalypses has increased to the point where academics and journalists who make it their business to cover modern millenarian timetables have had trouble keeping track of them all.

The relative reserve of Darby's approach seemed to have been overtaken by events. Mikhail Gorbachev's birthmark, for example, seemed incontrovertibly to be the mark of the beast (Rev 14:9). But changing political events have suggested differing identifications of the antichrist, and today there is an acknowledgment that there are *many* antichrists.[15] Yet getting the ultimate antichrist's identification straight is crucial, because there is a precise scenario, drawn from the Revelation, that is in the process of unfolding. Fortunately, on this view, the real identity of the whore of Babylon in Revelation 17 has allegedly been revealed:

> So when John saw this "woman" or apostate church "drunk with the blood of the saints," he was certainly not exaggerating. Even scores of Catholic writers have been mightily embarrassed about what their church practiced for hundreds of years. With the vast record now known—of priests sodomizing young men, of many popes openly maintaining mistresses and fathering illegitimate children all over Italy and high offices in the church being offered and bought for money—it has seemed to many objective historians that this powerful church was the veritable embodiment of evil in nearly every aspect.[16]

This then signals the most important of events in relation to the millennium:

> Soon, the ultimate personification of the Antichrist will appear on the world scene. Appearing at first as a kind and gentle "peace-maker," he will gradually assert more and more authority. His authority will be enhanced by the false miracles Satan performs through him (Rev 13:13). Then, the adoring masses will scream with excitement when they see him, and the doctrine of the Antichrist will permeate nearly all of professing Christianity—all except the "little flock" (Luke 12:32) described in Revelation 12:13-17.[17]

Evidently, with Gorbachev's removal from power and the dissolution of the Soviet Union, Dispensationalists encountered a degree of uncertainty. Where had the confirmation of their hopes gone? The strength of Darby's scheme had been its restraint. The rapture, while quickly unfolding, would not itself be an event whose starting date could be calculated beforehand. Divine intervention in Darby's mind was not historically conditioned.

But as we have seen, many Dispensationalists cast aside such reserve and committed themselves to actual dates. With this arises an obvious difficulty. If signs such as the rise of Israel and the threat of Soviet power demonstrated that the end was near, why does the rapture tarry? In 1982 the television evangelist Pat Robertson assured his viewers that "by the fall of 1982 there is going to be a judgment on the world," but later pulled back from this guarantee by declaring more equivocally that "there *can* be peace;

there *can* be plenty; there *can* be freedom."[18] Ambivalence became the order of the Dispensationalist day, even to the point that progressive views of the millennium were considered afresh.

Since the fall of the Soviet Union, those in search of signs of the coming rapture have shifted their gaze in significant numbers to Jerusalem, and predictions center on the imminent rebuilding of its ancient temple, destroyed by the Romans in 70 CE. In so doing they feed into one of the most volatile confrontations of our time.

The most well-known Dispensationalist predictions about the temple in recent times have come from the phenomenally successful author of apocalyptic fiction, Tim LaHaye (with Jerry B. Jenkins). Creator of the best-selling Left Behind series of the 1990s and 2000s, LaHaye portrays the Revelation of John as a forecast of how a new temple must be built in Jerusalem in order to provoke a war that will bring human civilization to an end prior to Jesus' return in glory.

The elaborate scenario imagined by LaHaye in his novels—adapted in a series of successful feature films—resolves a long-standing problem experienced by those who hold literally to apocalyptic readings of the New Testament. In the Synoptic Gospels Jesus appears to predict the destruction of the temple in Jerusalem and the subsequent coming of the cosmic Son of Man to judge all humanity (Matt 24–25; Mark 13; Luke 21). But while the Romans did indeed burn down Jerusalem and its temple in 70 CE, no judgment by the Son of Man followed. Why did the judgment not come if, as Fundamentalists believe, Scripture is infallible and if Jesus' prophecy were valid?

In their book *Desecration: Antichrist Takes the Throne,* Tim LaHaye and Jerry B. Jenkins set out as "the Truth behind the Fiction" of their work: that Jesus actually referred to the destruction of a *Third* Temple to be built in the future.[19] (The temple destroyed by the Romans was the Second Temple, which had been erected by Jews returning to their homeland after a long period of exile in Babylon. That exile had begun after the destruction of the First Jewish Temple in 586 BCE.) When that Third Temple is destroyed, the end would be truly upon us, for in the apocalyptic new Jerusalem there is no sacrificial temple left at all: "the Lord God, the Almighty, is the temple, and the Lamb" (Rev 21:22).

This is all part of the new heaven and new earth promised in the Apocalypse (21:1), which presupposes comprehensive and cosmic destruction during the course of divine judgment, and culminates in Jesus' coming as the Word of God described two chapters earlier (19:11-13). That cosmic disaster, also anticipated in the Synoptic Gospels, simply did not occur with the Roman arson of the temple in 70 CE. By resetting the apocalyptic clock of both the Revelation of John and the Synoptic Gospels to the erection of a Third Temple, their eschatological scenarios could be maintained.

Views such as LaHaye's attracted a small following in the first two decades after the establishment of the State of Israel, when anticipations of a Third Temple were marginal among Jews and Christians alike. But the Six-Day War of 1967, when Israel wrested control of east Jerusalem and the area of the Temple Mount from Jordan, changed everything. Israel's spectacular and unqualified military success, wholly unexpected, fueled Dispensationalist thinking among Christians. In the wake of the dissolution of the Soviet Union, LaHaye also shifted the identity of the antichrist from a Soviet leader to the secretary-general of the United Nations. In a post-rapture world, the UN oppresses those Christians left behind during the seven years John Nelson Darby had predicted between the rapture and the millennium. World government and globalization are aligned with Satan in this fresh pre-millennialist expectation, and Israel's progress toward building a Third Temple becomes a sign that the end is near.

Many Israelis also believed that their victory must have been the result of supernatural intervention. Jewish expectations concerning the Third Temple have become influential, although unlike their Christian counterparts, Jewish apocalypticists do not see the new temple as temporary. One young Israeli paratrooper in 1967, Israel Ariel, upon hearing the rumor that two old men were standing in the vicinity of the just-captured Temple Mount, told himself that they must be the Messiah and the Prophet Elijah.

"Who else would appear here during the battle of the Temple Mount after two thousand years?"[20]

Just as Puritan apocalypticists four centuries earlier had interpreted Elizabeth I's victory over the Spanish Armada as God's sign of triumph for his chosen, so Israel Ariel believed that "all the dispersed of Israel shall gather then and come to Jerusalem and to the Temple."[21] He even felt he could identify *two* heavenly witnesses of this truth, just as they appear in Revelation 11:3-4. Unlike the Revelation, however, Ariel foresaw a temple in Jerusalem on the grounds of military victory and the signs he saw.

Israel Ariel's reaction in the first flush of an unexpected military triumph was not an example of merely passing enthusiasm. His words in the paragraph above come from a prayer book he designed after the Six-Day War, when—as a rabbi and one time leader of the religious and nationalist Kach party, which has been banned in Israel—he defended the actions of the "Jewish Underground" which conspired unsuccessfully to blow up the mosques on the Temple Mount in 1984. The organization Ariel founded in 1987, The Temple Institute, developed a program dealing comprehensively with all practical matters involved in establishing a new temple:[22] questions of how to purify workers on the site with the ashes of a red heifer, regular and repeated sacrificial practice, the clothing of priests, the correct design of utensils, and methods of purification. This is a program for a permanent, hegemonic Israel to which all Jews return and the nations offer obedience.

Even as this Israeli Jewish movement for the Third Temple exacerbated tensions with local Muslims, it attracted the support of some Christians, especially in the United States. The affinity is natural, although the motivations involved are incommensurate. Nonetheless, pre-millenarian Christians have made common cause with a movement of millenarian Judaism. For the former, the aim is a temple that Christ will destroy prior to Christ's *parousia*; for the latter, the temple is the permanent throne of the Messiah to which all nations shall stream after their defeat.

The level of cooperation between these Jewish and Christian groups has been startling. On the Jewish side, the Temple Mount Faithful presents an open appeal for financial support on its electronic site: "all who have placed hope in the Scriptures and have faith in the One true G-d are invited to participate in the activities of the Temple Mount and Land of Israel Faithful Movement."[23] The head of the organization, Gershon Salomon, appeared with Pat Robertson on the Christian Broadcast Network's 700 Club in 1991 to target potential Christian donors in particular.[24]

The Temple Institute takes a similar approach, charging twenty-five dollars for membership, which grants free entry to their exhibition in Jerusalem and an inscription on a donors' wall, with the guarantee that "when the righteous messiah arrives he will seek out those who stood up in favor of the Holy Temple in order to reward them."[25] Cooperation between Jews who anticipate the Messiah and Fundamentalist Christians also extends to the mundane, such as the consultations between Rabbi Chaim Richman of the Temple Institute and the Reverend Clyde Lott, a Pentecostalist minister and cattle breeder, over the production of red heifers, which are necessary for purification within any new temple.[26]

The ready compatibility and active cooperation of premillennialist Christian Dispensationalism with temple-based Jewish messianism is one of the most significant developments in the modern appropriation of the Revelation of John. Dispensationalists can support the Third Temple as an edifice whose destruction will bring the end, while those who see the Third Temple as permanent nonetheless invoke the Revelation's Armageddon as the pivotal moment of all history.

Not surprisingly, cross-confessional support for the erection of a Third Temple does not extend to the third major faith community in the region. What Judaism calls the Temple Mount in Jerusalem is for Muslims al-Harim al-Sharif, the Noble Sanctuary. According to Islamic tradition, in 621 CE the Prophet traveled by night during a miraculous journey from Mecca to Jerusalem, and then journeyed into heaven. The Dome of the Rock and the al-Masjid al-Aqsa (the Furthest Mosque) delineate this sacred territory. The sanctity of the Harim al-Sharif does not rival that of the Kaba in Mecca; Jerusalem is usually reckoned as the third holy site in Islam, after Mecca and Medina. Yet the Harim al-Sharif remains territory of undeniable importance to Muslims. Jewish activity on the Temple Mount that appears supportive of the Third Temple project has repeatedly led to violence, for example in 2000 with the outbreak of the Al-Aqsa Intifada, when Ariel Sharon, then a candidate for prime minister, made a campaign visit to the Temple Mount with an armed escort.

This is not to say, however, that Muslims eschew millenarianism. The Quran, like the Hebrew Bible and the New Testament, includes a strongly eschatological dimension, and elements from the Revelation of John have featured in Muslim eschatology from the outset. The Surah called Al-Inshiqaq (numbered 84), "The Sundering," is so named for its opening line, with its reference to when the sky shall split, in the manner of Jewish and Christian apocalypses, in order to set the scene for a final judgment that includes punishment of the wicked and reward for the righteous in the same manner as Revelation 20–21.

Gog and Magog (Rev 29:8) also find their way into the Quran in a way that shows the influence of the Apocalypse. The Surah Al-Kahf, "The Cave," identifies Gog and Magog as the *ultimate* enemies of believers; they are kept out provisionally by a wall of supernatural power, but are ready to erupt at the last judgment (18:94-102).

The apocalyptic tradition of Islam is imbued with the Christian expectation of Jesus' place in final judgment as the following *hadith*, from the ninth-century CE collection of Abu al-Husayn Muslim, clearly shows:[27]

> Then Allah will send the Messiah, son of Mary, who will descend to the white minaret on the east side of Damascus, wearing two saffron-colored garments and placing his hands on the wings of two angels. When he lowers his head, beads of perspiration will fall from it, and when he raises it, beads like pearls will flow from it. Death will strike every infidel who breathes the odor of the Messiah, and breath will extend as far as he can see. Jesus will search for the Antichrist until the gate of Ludd, where he will kill him. (*al-Sahih* 4:2253–54)

There follows the extermination of Jews who do not convert.

Jesus' prayer for final victory then appears, directed against a familiar enemy:

> Jesus and his companions will beseech Allah and He will send insects to bite the people of Gog and Magog in the neck, so that in the morning they will all be dead. Jesus and his companions will come down and will find every corner and recess of the earth filled with the stench of their putrefaction. They will pray again to Allah, who will send birds that resemble the necks of camels. They will snatch up the bodies of Gog and Magog and throw them where Allah wishes. Allah will send rains that no house or tent can keep out and in this way the earth will be washed so thoroughly that it will look like a mirror. (*al-Sahih* 4:2254)

In light of this background, contemporary Muslim appropriations of the Revelation of John are neither aberrant nor surprising. Recent apocalyptic contributions nonetheless remain stunning for their bold claim, not only to subvert Christian Zionist claims, but also to make *better* sense of the Revelation than Dispensationalists do. In a pamphlet that appeared in response to the second Intifada in 2000, Shaykh Shafar al-Hawali—at one time a professor at Umm al-Qura University in Mecca who became radicalized by the introduction of American troops in Saudi Arabia after the first war against Saddam Hussein—attacked President George W. Bush, together with the Reverends Jerry Falwell, Pat Robertson, and Jimmy Swaggart, for their stance against Islam as if *they* were the instantiations of Gog and Magog.

In al-Hawali's apocalypse,[28] Jesus is the Messiah, while the false prophets are Paul and the popes, the beast presents any form of Zionism, and Babylon is the West. Clearly, al-Hawali had become familiar not only with the book of Revelation but had imbibed the tradition of Protestant commentary from the time of the Reformation, particularly in its attack on the papacy. In this way Armageddon entered the vocabulary of militant Islam after the invasion of Afghanistan in 2001, enabled by Arabic-language publishers such as the Cairo-based Dar al-Kitab al-Arabi, which has flourished over the last decade by producing both apocalyptic tracts and refutations of them.

This Revelation-inspired style of apocalyptic thinking has by no means been embraced by the majority of Muslim religious leaders and thinkers. Critics have attacked al-Hawali and his tract *The Days of Wrath* as "deviant and treacherous" because he absorbed the methods of the *Kuffaar*, that is, unbelievers.[29] Salafism, a traditionalist movement within Islam frequently identified in the West with aggressive *jihad*, is quite capable of turning against the new apocalypticism precisely because it is new and foreign.

Revelation-inspired apocalypse has also been criticized from within the Christian Fundamentalist tradition. In a scathing rebuttal of Tim LaHaye's Dispensationalism, Hank Hanegraaff—a conservative evangelical broadcaster and writer—has recently argued that to read in 1 Thessalonians 4, spliced into the Revelation, "a paradigm in which two-thirds of the Jewish people will shortly be eradicated in a holocaust massacre while Jesus' people relax in heavenly mansions is a frightful imposition."[30] Even more frightful, in his view, is the Third Temple movement:

> Failure to interpret Scripture in the light of Scripture creates a genuine conundrum for Christian Zionists. If temple sacrifices in the Millennium are efficacious for ceremonial uncleanness, Christ's atonement on the cross was insufficient to pay for all sin for all time.[31]

Here Hanegraaff goes beyond an ad hominem onslaught on Tim LaHaye, and attempts to wrest Fundamentalism away from Dispensationalism. The insistence upon Scripture's infallible consistency remains; in fact, it is stressed in order to show that the inventive insertions by Dispensationalists betray the Fundamentalist axioms.

Yet Israel Ariel and thinkers like him have had a profound impact on the religion and politics of Israel. The Temple Mount site remains a point of increasing tension. Should Israel continue to insist on both formal and operational authority over the area to the exclusion of Islam's engagement with the site, then with or without the influence of teachers such as al-Hawali, it is difficult to imagine Palestinians and the surrounding Muslim nations agreeing to live in peace with their Jewish neighbors. This conclusion has already been reached within Israel, where a growing number of civic and religious leaders in the majority Jewish community have taken politicians to task for accommodating messianic expectations.[32]

In nonpolitical, religious terms, Rabbi David Hartman has met the challenge of renewed millenarianism after the Six-Day War by arguing for a new definition of messianism altogether. Instead of disputing the details of prediction, he builds on the theology of Maimonides, arguing that "events in history need not be appreciated only as signposts that point to a new eschatological future and mark the progress of God's redemptive purpose. Historical events can become religiously significant to the degree that they bear witness to the foundational moments of the Jewish tradition."[33]

There is no reason to assume that Hartman will single-handedly change the course of messianic thinking in Judaism, any more than that Hanegraaff will alter the trajectory of Fundamentalism away from Dispensationalism, or that al-Hawali's Salafist critics will make Muslims rethink their counter-Dispensationalism. After all, both the positions described here and their counterpositions represent only a sample of a vibrant, often contentious, and frequently confusing set of arguments concerning the human future. The fact of that diversity within religious traditions shows that the militant application of Dispensationalism is far from inevitable. The Revelation can certainly be read as predicting catastrophe and combat; but that is not a necessary interpretation.

Further Reading

Scholarship on this topic is vast, but accessible works include Paul Boyer, *When Time Shall Be No More: Prophecy Belief in Modern American Culture* (Cambridge, Mass.: Belknap, 1992); Stephen D. O'Leary, *Arguing the Apocalypse: A Theory of Millennial Rhetoric* (New York: Oxford University Press, 1994); David L. Rowe, *God's Strange Work: William Miller and the End of the World* (Grand Rapids: Eerdmans, 2008); Eugen Weber, *Apocalypses: Prophecies, Cults, and Millennial Beliefs through the Ages* (Cambridge, Mass.: Harvard University Press, 1999); Tim LaHaye and Jerry B. Jenkins, *Are We Living in the End Times?* (Carol Stream, Ill.: Tyndale House, 2011); Torin Monahan, "Marketing the Beast: *Left Behind* and the Apocalypse Industry," *Media, Culture & Society* 30, no. 6 (2008): 813–30; Motti Inbari,

Jewish Fundamentalism and the Temple Mount: Who Will Build the Third Temple? trans. Shaul Vardi (Albany: State University of New York Press, 2009); Ehud Sprinzak, *The Ascendance of Israel's Radical Right* (New York: Oxford University Press, 1991); Grant R. Jeffrey, *Armageddon: The Earth's Last Days* (Wheaton, Ill.: Tyndale House, 1997); and Jean-Pierre Filiu, *Apocalypse in Islam*, trans. M. B. DeBevoise (Berkeley: University of California Press, 2011).

7

Visions in Patmos, and Beyond

> I witness to everyone who hears the words of the prophecy of this scroll: If anyone adds to them, God will add to him the plagues written in this scroll. And if anyone takes away from the words of the scroll of this prophecy, God will take away his share from the tree of life and from the Holy City, which are written in this scroll.
>
> Revelation 22:18-19

Religious vision involves not only what is seen. In the Apocalypse the experience explicitly includes what is heard. During John's opening vision (1:11-13) he first hears a voice, identifying itself as "the alpha and omega, the first and the last." In an emblematic statement, John says that he turned "to see the voice." That is when John first sees Jesus as the Son of Man, the judge of all beings. Although the visual element in the Apocalypse is the most vivid, the auditory provides meaning, guides interpretation, and links John's vision to key biblical insights such as those in Isaiah (Isa 41:4, 6; 48:12): God standing as the first and the last.

Vision refers to an experience of the transcendent in the setting of a specified context, such that the seer reports that the conditions of this world correspond to elements of higher reality. For that reason, none of the types of interpretation we have considered can be rejected out of hand, because they come to grips seriously, not only with specific passages, but also with a sense of the Apocalypse as a whole.

Until recently, academic investigation has treated vision as if it were ornamental. That attitude was an artifact of the Enlightenment's distrust of perceptions that could not be verified empirically. But within the worlds of Judaism and Christianity, visions conveyed truths more secure than the senses ordinarily report, and meditation was more journey than rest. The Revelation of John proposes such a journey, taking the hearer from the position of listening to angelic messages in the opening chapters, to entering through an opening to heaven at chapter 4, and from there encountering celestial realities. From the time that John of Patmos called attention to the open door of heaven, he invited hearers and readers to join in the vision.

Vision is what binds together the thousand years of Papias, Augustine's celebration of transcendent power, the anticipation of Spirit by Joachim, the zeal practiced by Luther, the restraint of Isaac Newton, and John Nelson Darby's hope of the rapture. A reading of the Revelation that set aside any of those interpretations would ignore key aspects of the text, and pass over vital developments of spirituality in the West.

Yet in each case, a tendency was clearly at work to claim an exclusive right to interpret the text, on the grounds of an interpretation that effectively added to what John of Patmos said, or subtracted from it. That is just what John did not want to happen.

Perhaps John of Patmos understood or intuited that, for a vision to maintain its integrity, it must not seek confirmation in this broken world. Rather, a wise interpreter remains engaged and expectant in tracing how the perception of meaning relates to and influences the unfolding of events. In taking this stance, John staked out a position within the apocalyptic tradition that had unfolded long before his time.

The Apocalyptic Genre

Visions in the Hebrew Bible are often associated with the temple. During sacrifice there, Isaiah describes seraphim crying out, "Holy, holy, holy, Yahweh of armies, the whole earth is full of his glory"

(Isa 6:3), words that were adapted by John of Patmos (Rev 4:8). Sacrificial worship, with all its emotional engagement with rituals that ranged from penance to celebration, became a natural setting for vision, understood as a sensory and cognitive perception of higher reality.

The destruction of the temple of Solomon (the First Temple) by the Babylonians in 586 BCE did not bring visionary experience to an end. Rather, hopes for the restoration of worship on Mount Zion were expressed in vivid, visual terms in biblical works such as Ezekiel and the book of Zechariah. In the absence of God's throne on earth, Ezekiel 1 and Zechariah 3 portray that reality in heaven. Confidence that God would finally restore his presence on the ground was confirmed with the establishment of the Second Temple by the end of the sixth century BCE. But when the Seleucid monarch Antiochus IV seized the temple for pagan worship in the second century BCE, the apocalyptic model emerged fully as a literature of resistance centered on the restoration of Israel's worship in the temple.

Apocalyptic prophecy was typically attributed to a figure in the distant past. For example, the biblical book of Daniel's putative author lived centuries before the Seleucid crisis; he therefore appeared to predict events accurately until the time that the apocalypse was written during the second century BCE. The failure of their predictions after the period of their composition permits apocalypses to be dated. Pseudonymity—in this case, attribution to Daniel, a Babylonian figure made to "predict" the Seleucid crisis—is a characteristic of apocalyptic writing. Daniel's apocalypse involved surreal, sequential images, whose meaning was explained by angelic intervention from the heavenly court through the pseudonymous author. The impact of the whole was designed to provide authoritative hope and the resolve to assure the temple's restoration, when judgment is given to "one like a son of man" (Dan 7:13), the heavenly representative of Israel.

The Revelation of John is committed to the world of heavenly vision, to what the seer sees and hears beyond this world, as well as to interaction with the heavenly court of angels. These fundamental components of apocalypse are depicted in searing detail, reflecting a deep commitment to these elements and a determined drive to interpret the meaning of what is seen and heard. In fact, heavenly seeing, heavenly hearing, and engagement with angels—judged in terms of the proportion of the text they cover and their intensity—are pressed to a new level in the Revelation as compared to Daniel and other apocalypses. At the same time, John of Patmos takes up scriptural antecedents: that seraphic hymn of Isaiah, the throne visions of Ezekiel and Zechariah, as well as the identification of God's agent of judgment as "son of man."

The relationship of the Revelation to other literary apocalypses does not indicate uniformity within the genre. Scholars originally designated apocalyptic literature as such on the grounds of similarity to the canonical Apocalypse, the Revelation of John. Once this apocalyptic genre was recognized, the Revelation no longer appeared unique, but joined works in the Pseudepigrapha (noncanonical but widely read books) such as *Enoch* and *Jubilees*, as well as 2 Esdras in the Apocrypha (works in the Christian version of the Scriptures of Israel, but not in the Hebrew canon), and the *War of the Sons of Light Against the Sons of Darkness* among the Dead Sea Scrolls. Recent discoveries show that the genre was extensive; apocalyptic writing and thinking emerged as part and parcel of early Judaism as well as of early Christianity.

With the recognition of the genre, there came the realization that Judaism was capable of powerful hopes for the end of oppression and the opening of a messianic era of vindication. Looking beyond the Hebrew canon—and considering the Apocrypha, the Pseudepigrapha, and the collection of works discovered at Qumran near the Dead Sea in 1947—enabled scholars to map more accurately how Jews of the Second Temple period viewed the world, history, and humanity.

Apocalypses sometimes carry the encoded equivalent of a sell-by date: the moment when the author has to speak, not of the future of the putative seer, but his own future. In the case of first-century works, the temple's destruction and claims that it would soon be restored usually indicate this date. But John of Patmos does not see the temple's restoration as part of the prophetic future; the temple is lost as a datable point of reference, because its enduring *absence* is predicted. One of his signature ideas—expressed on the basis of his consistent identification of Jesus as the celestial Lamb—is that, although there will a new Jerusalem, there will not be a temple there "because the Lord God Almighty is the temple, and the Lamb" (21:22).

John engages in allusions so cryptic that their references have been open to persistent debate. This difficulty produces frustration when one reads the Revelation alongside other apocalyptic works. Apocalypses usually exercise care to include identifiable, if typically puzzling, references to the destruction or desecration of the temple. When those dreadful events are "predicted" by a "Daniel," their prophecies of the restoration of the temple become much more powerful and convincing. But why should the Revelation anchor itself in the time of the temple, when its basic insistence is that no physical temple will be included in the millennial rule of the saints and the new Jerusalem that is to follow? John's revision of the usual apocalyptic scenario, targeted on the restoration of the temple, caused him to refer to the past in ways that are difficult to understand. The apocalyptic calendar of the Revelation is as elusive as the identity of the beast whose number is 666 (Rev 13:18) or the seven heads of the beast (17:10) or even the identity of John himself. Understanding why the book engages in a heightened level of elusiveness is key to its interpretation. The question of authorship will occupy us next, and then the meaning of John's visions.

The Issue of Authorship

The force and diversity of the Revelation's impact after its composition reflects the power of its author's vision. John's identity has been a matter of discussion and dispute, presenting another facet of the interpretative life of the Revelation. The name "John," from the Aramaic *Yochanan*, was common during the first century. Was the author who says he saw visions and heard divine voices on the island of Patmos off the coast of present-day Turkey (Rev 1:9-20) the same as the author of the Gospel according to John? Irenaeus (writing in 180 CE) asserted that, although the Revelation was recently composed, near the end of the reign of Domitian (who died in 96 CE), it was authored by the apostle John, who lived to a surprisingly old age (*Against Heresies* 5.30.3). Irenaeus' identification of John of Patmos with the author of the Fourth Gospel has been criticized since antiquity: the Revelation and John's Gospel are as different in content as they are in style.

Yet as applied to the seer of Patmos, "John" *does not seem to be a pseudonym at all.* In the Hebrew Bible, Daniel is without question pseudonymous, attributed to a Babylonian sage who lived centuries before the book in his name was produced, while the apocalyptic additions to Ezekiel, Isaiah, and Zechariah were appended to the original books identified with those names. Second Esdras in the Apocrypha, as well as *Enoch* in the Pseudepigrapha, fits within the pattern of claiming authorship by a seer from the ancient past in order to increase the inherent authority of the apocalypse and to make its predictions accurate—at least from the time of the putative seer until the moment of writing. But the Revelation of John, from the point of view of pseudonymity, a well-established characteristic of genre, is slippery.

Attribution to an apostle, John the son of Zebedee, became conventional from the time of Justin Martyr during the second century (*Dialogue with Trypho* 81.4), when he espoused the Revelation's prediction of a millennium of the saints on earth, making a case for including the Revelation within the canon at a time when apostolic authorship was thought to be a qualification. But no reference to the author *in the text* of the Revelation connects him to the son of Zebedee, or to his brother James. The author simply calls himself "John" (*Ioannes,* Rev 1:9)—a Hellenized form of the common Semitic name *Yochanan*—and says he was on the island of Patmos off the southwest coast of Asia Minor. Any connection with Galilee, from which John and James the sons of Zebedee originated, seems implausible. An attempt has been made to argue that the author is John the Baptist,[1] in that he preached judgment and in John's Gospel called Jesus "the Lamb of God" (1:29, 36). These connections are striking, but they have been held by most commentators to reflect more the common prophetic background of John the Baptist and the Apocalypse than John's authorship, since events well after John the Baptist's death appear to be in view.

In any case, even the Gospel according to John does not actually name its author, so that its connection to John *the son of Zebedee*, still conventional in some circles, is open to doubt and debate. Within New Testament scholarship, discussion of who wrote the Fourth Gospel is a cottage industry. Indeed, routine reference to it as "the Fourth Gospel" shows how deep uncertainty in regard to authorship is. Other candidates include a presbyter named John from Asia Minor, Apollos (Paul's rival from Alexandria; 1 Cor 3:4–4:6; Acts 18:24–19:7), Mary Magdalene, the disciple Nathaniel, and even Lazarus.

Whoever wrote the Gospel, the text is written in what has been recognized since antiquity as a totally different style from the Revelation. Once the Revelation was written, its author could be identified with any first-century author named "John" who could be plausibly associated with Patmos, but the text actually made no such identification. There is no trace of the careful identification of the putative author one finds in, for example, Daniel and 2 Esdras, and the scarified, poetic rhythm of the Gospel according to John contrasts with the ornate, repetitive hymns, rhetorical prose, and sometime ill-constructed grammar in the Revelation.

John's Visions
Their Meaning and Setting

The author tells of how the risen Jesus came to him on the island of Patmos during worship on Sunday, the Lord's Day (1:1-9), commissioning John to write seven letters to each of seven churches (1:10–3:22) in Asia Minor. This commission is built into the outset of the book, which says that it is "Jesus Christ's apocalypse, which God gave to him to show his servants what must happen in haste, and he signaled it, sending through his angel to his servant, John" (Rev 1:1). The seven churches in Asia Minor correspond to the seven spirits that are before God's throne (1:4), an early indication that the number seven is a structural principle that will be developed throughout the book.

In ancient Hebrew, Babylonian, and Persian numerology, seven represents totality—the rhythm in Genesis of creation and repose. Israelite fascination with the number represents a version of Babylonian wisdom, rooted in the observation of the heavens. In the lunar calendars of the ancient Near East, the seven-day week marked the phases of the moon: four quarters waxing and waning during the month. Israel embraced this calendar, and Genesis embeds the seven-day week in the structure of nature itself (Gen 1:3–2:3). An earlier apocalyptic work, the *Book of Enoch* (chapters 72–82), also features seven as a principle of cosmological order, even though it sustains an argument for an innovative calendar.

In the Apocalypse, seven is the number of completion, not only of creation, but of the judgment that is to come, because God is alpha and omega, "who is and was and is to come, the almighty" (Rev 1:7-8). That climaxes the preface of the book, after which John identifies himself with his readers "in the tribulation and kingdom and endurance in Jesus," explaining that the Word of God and the witness of Jesus had brought him to the island of Patmos, just off the coast from Ephesus (1:9).

The term "tribulation" (*thlipsis*) is mistranslated as "persecution" in the New Revised Standard Version, but what John writes to the seven churches shows that he does not simply equate tribulation with official persecution. This mistake in translation suggests that scholars have wished to see more evidence of persecution in the Apocalypse than it actually presents. John confronts more complicated challenges than unqualified persecution from the state.

In writing to the seven churches (Ephesus, Smyrna, Pergamon, Thyatira, Sardis, Philadelphia, and Laodicea), John sometimes alludes to the difficulties they face. In Ephesus, false apostles (2:2); in Smyrna, defamation from the "synagogue of Satan" (2:9); in Pergamon, martyrdom (2:13) and false teaching (2:14-15) in the city where "Satan dwells" on his throne; in Thyatira, a seductress styled as Jezebel who encourages fornication and eating meat sacrificed to idols (2:20); and varying degrees of faintheartedness in the last three—Sardis, Philadelphia, and Laodicea (3:1-22).

Martyrdom is mentioned, but only in the case of Antipas in Pergamon (2:13), and false teaching and lack of enthusiasm are the most frequent problems cited. The root of scholars' surmise that persecution is the setting of the Apocalypse is less the challenges actually cited than the content of visions: martyrs moaning for vindication beneath the heavenly altar (Rev 6:10), vials of divine wrath leading to Armageddon (16:16), and the annihilation of Babylon (17:1–19:5). Images of this kind caused some commentators to presume a setting of overt and Empire-wide persecution, but Roman policy did not become oppressive to that extent until centuries after the Apocalypse was written. The tension between experience on earth and the promises of heaven is produced less by a particular edict of government than by the seer's realization of how far his world is from the new Jerusalem.

The issue most plainly addressed in the letters to the seven churches is far from global: the question of animals sacrificed to idols, *eidolothuta* (Rev 2:14, 20). A decree of James the brother of Jesus in the book of Acts, endorsed by an apostolic meeting, prohibits the consumption of such food, along with fornication (and blood, a basic prohibition in the rules of *kashrut*; Acts 15:13-22). The pairing of idolatry and fornication is as old as the figure of Jezebel, whose evil deeds and violent end stand in counterpoint to the great Hebrew prophets Elijah and Elisha (1 Kgs 16:31–2 Kgs 9). The connection to Jezebel surfaces in Revelation 2:20, linked, not with any imperial edict, but with an alleged "prophetess" in Thyatira. The zealous insistence upon the apostolic decree is fierce; branded with the lurid image of Jezebel, the unnamed prophetess and her followers are consigned to death (2:22-23)—for pollution, rather than persecution.

John of Patmos also calls his opponents "the synagogue of Satan" (2:9-10; 3:9). They are accused of a "blasphemy" (*blasphemia*)—or defamation—that enables the devil to imprison some believers in Smyrna; John asserts that members of this congregation "say they are Jews and are not." Perhaps John is denying the title of Jews to other Jews for a theological motivation, such as their refusal of the message of Christ, or their denunciation of followers of Jesus to Roman magistrates. But maybe he refers to

"God-fearers" (Gentile sympathizers with Judaism), or to assimilated Jews who in John's judgment acceded too much to Greco-Roman practice, especially in regard to food sacrificed to idols. It might even be that "the synagogue of Satan" should be associated with the practice of *eidolothuta* among other followers of Jesus. In principle Paul accepted the consumption of foods sacrificed to idols (1 Cor 8); are his congregations in view, and was "Jezebel" his prophet?

The identification of Pergamon as "where Satan dwells" (Rev 2:13) may point in this direction. Whatever idolatry the satanic throne refers to, a pagan cult is evidently in view. The most likely reference is to a monumental sacrificial site, presently in the Pergamon Museum in Berlin, which sits atop a frieze of the battle between the giants and the gods of Olympus. John would then be answering that heroic battle with his own account of war in heaven. In any case, just after the reference to Satan's throne in Pergamon, John refers to the teaching of Balaam, and also links that to eating food sacrificed to idols (2:14). It has been suggested that Balaam is a symbol for Paul.[2] Although that suggestion is possible, after Paul's death those of his followers who produced the Pastoral Epistles turned him into a proponent of keeping the law, and they characterized antinomians as false prophets (1 Tim 1). "Balaam" seems to be a cipher for a more radical reading of Paul than the Pastoral Epistles promote.

Whichever of these options is best for understanding "synagogue of Satan," Roman persecutors are not in view, although John does threaten opponents with violence. The Son of Man promises to throw Jezebel and those who commit adultery with her into a bed of great tribulation, and to "kill her children with death" (Rev 2:22-23). There is no explaining away the violence of imagery in the Apocalypse as a response to Roman persecution. It is rather the continuation, and enhancement, of prophetic oracles of judgment that are part and parcel of the scriptural tradition.

After the letters to the seven churches, the visionary scene shifts. Instead of the seer opening his eyes to Christ's presence on earth, he looks into heaven itself, invited to enter an open gate or door to see the throne of God in heaven, where Christ appears as a slain Lamb and as a Lion (4:1–5:14). The seer no longer sees heavenly realities on earth, but looks into the secrets of heaven itself, where angelic worship echoing the temple liturgy in Jerusalem surrounds the divine throne in powerful contrast to the throne of Satan in Pergamon.

This Lamb that is also a Lion alone has standing to unseal a scroll, mentioned at the opening of the vision of the throne (5:1), in which human fate is inscribed. As he removes each of seven seals, disasters are unleashed and enumerated (6:1–8:6). What stands behind the first six seals is detailed, but a vision of those who are saved interrupts the introduction of the seventh seal; this seventh seal will then ramify into seven further angels with seven trumpets. The reader or hearer is to focus more and more on heaven, through a sequenced pattern of sevens, until heaven, at the end of the book, comes to earth.

The first four disasters unleashed from the open seals, the famous horseman of the Apocalypse, relate to dangers all too familiar in the history of Asia Minor:

1. A conquering archer on a white horse (6:1-2)
2. An armed rider on a red horse, removing peace (6:3-4)
3. A rider on a black horse, imposing prices for wheat and barley (6:5-6)
4. Death on a pale horse, with power to slay by human and natural means (6:7-8).

The third horseman may appear anticlimactic compared to the others, but economic travail is part of John's world. The enigmatic reference to spare the wine at the end of verse 6 may refer to a situation under Emperor Domitian. He had ordered the destruction of vineyards in order to enable more grain to be planted; when he rescinded the order, there was cause for celebration. Whether or not John alludes to Domitian's orders in particular, the realism of the crises envisaged remains evident.

Beginning with the fifth seal, however, the scene reverts to heaven, taking up the throne vision in chapter 4. Now the focus is on the altar before the throne, and to the souls of the martyrs beneath it (6:9-11). They ask how long they must wait for vindication, and the answer comes back that their full number must first be achieved. The sixth seal's opening imagines that number fulfilled, with earthquake and cosmological dissolution confronting the wealthy and powerful with the wrath of the Lamb (6:12-17).

Before the climax of this judgment with the seventh seal, the Apocalypse breaks in with its vision of those who are to be saved. To do so, seals are not opened; instead seals are *applied* to 144,000 of Israel (12,000 from each clan; Rev 7:1-8). Then a numberless host from all nations (7:9-14) joins in the worship of God and the Lamb and in the vindication of those who whitened their robes in the blood of the Lamb (7:14).

Although this vision interrupts the unsealing of the seventh seal, it does so strategically, resuming the throne vision and setting out the purpose of the prophecies that follow from this point. The earthquake and the dissolution of the heavens when the sixth seal is released (6:12, 14) pick up imagery attributed to Jesus in his "little apocalypse" in the Synoptic Gospels (Matt 24:29; Mark 13:24-25; and especially Luke 21:11, 25). John of Patmos seems to key his unfolding visions to that moment, so that he provides both prequel and sequel by means of his visions. For this reason, the half hour of silence in heaven that follows is explicable, marking a caesura before the appearance of seven angels with seven trumpets that the unsealing of the seventh seal brings (8:1-2; cf. 1:10). Their release realizes the plea of the martyrs, and reference back to the heavenly throne and prayers of the saints pursues this theme (8:3-5).

The disasters unfolding through the prophecies of seven trumpets now power in from heaven and are described in surreal terms. The first four are terrible, but an angel marks the last three as worse, and they are far more detailed:

1. Hail and fire fall from heaven, mixed with blood (8:7).
2. A burning mountain is cast into the sea, turning one third to blood (8:8-9).
3. The star Absinth turns a third of fresh water to blood (8:10-11).

4. Darkness smites sun, moon, and stars, taking one third of their light (8:12).
5. A star opens a bottomless abyss, releasing monstrous locusts (9:1-12).
6. The sixth angel releases four destroying angels from the Euphrates which kill a third of humanity with an army of two hundred thousand mounted on monstrous horses (9:13-21).
7. The rule of the earth passes to the Lord and his Messiah, opening the temple in heaven; lightning, thunder, earthquake, and great hail emanate from the ark (11:14-19).

Between the sixth and the seventh trumpets the visionary interruption is considerably longer than the pause between the sixth and seventh seals. That longer caesura (of nearly two chapters) also marks a change in the visionary idiom of the Apocalypse.

Because the seventh trumpet will mark the completion of "the mystery of God" (10:7), an angel provides a book to the prophet that he ingests in order to prophesy again (10:1-11). The next chapter is perhaps the most puzzling in the book (11:1-13). The prophet is commanded, in the manner of Ezekiel before him (Ezek 40:1–43:17), to measure out the temple. It has been argued that Revelation 11:2 assumes that the temple is still standing, but that argument falters on the fact that Ezekiel, the model of John's vision, prophesied fourteen years after the destruction of Jerusalem, and yet also measured that sacred place (Ezel 40:1). A visionary temple does not require the existence of the physical sanctuary for it to be described.

Following this reference, "two witnesses" are promised, who are to prophesy with supernatural powers for a period of three and a half years (11:3-6), after which "the beast that ascends from the abyss will make war with them and conquer them and kill them," a reference which only becomes clear later, when the number of the beast is given as 666, Nero Caesar (11:7), the numerical values of whose name amount to that sum. He exposes the witnesses' bodies in "the great city," which is Rome, but "called spiritually Sodom and Egypt, where their Lord was crucified" (11:8).

Mention of Jesus' crucifixion has caused enormous confusion, in the attempt to identify the "great city" as Jerusalem, rather than Rome. But John here names unjust power, as he says, "spiritually": the location is no more literal than the references to Sodom and Egypt. John sees Rome as the authority behind the crucifixion just as Nero was behind the deaths of the two witnesses, who on this reading appear to have been Paul and Peter, both of whom died during Nero's pogrom after the great fire in Rome in 64 CE. Their ascent to heaven and vindication (11:9-13) is the trigger for the sounding of the seventh trumpet.

This visionary caesura includes heaven, but it is not restricted to the heavenly realm, as sometimes occurs earlier in the Revelation. Rather, the witnesses and the beast are earthly figures who become heavenly signs, as the temple in heaven is opened to signal the climax of the book in its second half: the reconciliation of heaven and earth.

Although this reconciliation is definitive, it is also violent, for both earth and heaven. Seven signs signal the persecution of the church [1], portrayed as a woman clothed with the sun (12:1-6, 13-16), by a dragon [2] representing the Roman Empire (12:3-17). At this stage, the careful architecture of seven is so strong that it no longer needs to be spelled out. But the signs follow inexorably, through [3] the beast from the sea (13:1-10), [4] the beast from the earth (13:11-18; with the signature number 666), [5] the Lamb (14:1-13), [6] the Son of Man (14:14-20), and finally [7] seven angels with the last plagues (15:1). The strife among these forces is so great as to amount to a "war in heaven" (12:7), and the defeat of the dragon in heaven—also identified as the devil and Satan—only makes him more vicious on earth (12:9).

Just before the release of the last angels and their plagues, another vision of worship in heaven intervenes: the Song of Moses and of the Lamb (15:2-8). The close of this scene is telling for the message of the Revelation as a whole: "no one could enter the temple until the seven plagues of the seven angels were completed." Heaven itself requires events on earth, reminiscent of the plagues of Exodus but more terrible, to purge the evil that had originated in heaven with Satan's rebellion:

1. Boils (16:2)
2. Sea turned to blood (16:3)
3. Rivers and fountains turned to blood (16:4-7)
4. Scorching of the sun (16:8-9)
5. Darkness from the beast's throne (16:10-11)
6. Euphrates dried up for Armageddon (16:12-16)
7. Earthquake and hail (16:17-21).

With these plagues out from the temple and finished, the last seven events of the book—not enumerated but structured to complement the work as a whole—unfold to arrive at their climax. In the first four, the whore of Babylon is defeated (17:1–19:5); the Wedding of the Lamb is announced (19:6-10); the conquering Word of God defeats all enemies (19:11-21), and the millennium of the saints follows (20:1-6). Even the climax of the millennium, however, does not end the heavenly war. Satan has been bound, but after a thousand years he is released, resulting in the last three events, the war of Gog and Magog (20:7-10), the final judgment (20:11-15), and the new Jerusalem (21:1–22:6).

John concludes his book (22:7-21) with a solemn warning not to tamper with it in any way. The text conveys power in its cadences as well as in its visions. At one level, the warning not to change John's wording (22:18-19) is surprising, since the Revelation's Greek is basic—on occasion to the point of being formally ungrammatical. These mistakes are so obvious that they sometimes appear deliberate. In addition to employing a form of the Koine dialect that took his message out of the literary mainstream, the author called special attention to some of what he said by means of disruptions in the expected grammar. Either directly or as artifice, these disruptions represent an underlying Semitic grammar that interrupts the normal flow of Greek.

Although interpreting the Revelation has been as difficult as it has proven controversial, its thematic interest in human events as conditioned by heavenly events is patent. Moreover, the architectural sequence of sevens indicates that heaven does not immediately seize the direction of history on earth, but proceeds by a dialectical interplay of visions and events. The length of these sequences has inclined a majority of commentators to opt for a

Domitianic dating, but that choice is perhaps incidental to the question of how to see the significance of John's approach.

Dating the Apocalypse of John

Writing during the fourth century, the historian Eusebius refers to deep disagreement in regard to the authorship of the Revelation, but he accepts Irenaeus' statement that it was composed during the reign of Domitian (*History of the Church* 3.18, 23-25). Eusebius then develops the influential view that the Apocalypse was written during a period of severe persecution. As he sees it, the beast whose number is 666 (Rev 13:18) is the Emperor Nero, and Domitian was that beast revived (Rev 13:12), returning to torture the saints again.

The identification of the beast with Nero has been widely accepted. The letters in the Hebrew alphabet stand for numbers, as well as sounds, and "Neron Caesar" in Hebrew or Aramaic adds up to the number 666 (or 616, depending upon variants in orthography also reflected in the manuscript tradition). The Semitic linguistic and cultural background of the Apocalypse is evident, and when John of Patmos says the number 666 represents "wisdom" and calls for "mind" (13:18), he encourages the shift to a Semitic enumeration. John calls for a mind with wisdom again in chapter 17, when he explains the meaning of the multiheaded monster of his vision: "The seven heads are seven mountains on which the woman is seated, they are also seven kings, five of whom have fallen, one is, and the other has yet to come" (Rev 17:9-10). Counting from Julius Caesar would make Nero the sixth king, followed by the short-lived reigns of Galba in 68 CE and Otho in 69 CE. Since Julius Caesar was not actually named emperor, the count might better be started with Augustus, his adoptive son, but that merely brings us to the eight-month reign of Vitellius, also in the year 69 CE.

Attempts have been made to skip over the reigns of some emperors, and so to bring John's enumeration down to the time of Domitian in order to coincide with Irenaeus' dating, but they appear artificial. On a straightforward reading, the beast whose number is 666, Nero Caesar, is a key figure in the Revelation of John. That has led to the argument that the Revelation as a whole was written before the destruction of the temple by the Romans in 70 CE.

This argument presupposes that John on the island of Patmos knew almost immediately (and simultaneously) of events in Rome and events in Jerusalem. But the way he refers to those two cities rather suggests a retrospective point of view. The woman seated on the beast in chapter 17 is identified: she is "Babylon the great, the mother of whores and of the abominations of the earth" (17:5)—a cipher for Rome, the city founded on seven hills (17:9), described as drunk on the blood of the martyrs of Jesus (17:6). Those martyrs allude to Rome from the time of Nero, who was the first major persecutor of Christians according to the Roman historian Tacitus. But the association of Rome with Babylon suggests a period after 70 CE, when Rome destroyed the Second Temple much as Babylon had destroyed the First Temple in 586 BCE. A setting well after 70 CE is also suggested by the seer's vision of the new Jerusalem: "And I did not see a temple in it because the Lord God Almighty is its temple, and the Lamb" (Rev 21:22). This vision seems to come from a time when the Second Temple was known to have been destroyed, and when worship of Jesus as the Lamb who was slain, understood as coregnant with God, took the place of sacrifice in the minds of many Christians (Rev 5:1-14).

Although a dating within the reign of Domitian remains the view of most major commentators, a date just prior to 70 CE has also found several recent defenders. The Revelation is a text of vision, and for that reason events of the author's past *and* present, as well as his expectations for the future, feature in his descriptions. Because John presents his work as visions, with only allusive historical content, dating the Revelation is a matter of inference. Once the visions are assessed as a structural whole, inference becomes more plausible.

Those who have learned by experience that our world is passing away, that what seemed stable is fragile, that what claims to be just might be destructive, can learn from the Revelation. Precisely because it includes the dark, retributive side of human anxiety, and because the book itself has been an instrument of theologies and policies that have provoked violence, the Revelation shows that visions of God, focused by means of those scriptural images that convey divine reality in its ambivalent power, reward scrutiny and critical attention.

The integrity of those visions requires faithful transmission and grappling with vision as vision, rather than as code or calendar or plan of battle. Neither adding to nor subtracting from John's words (Rev 22:18-19) means taking his rugged expression of what he calls "signs" (12:1, 3; 15:1) for what they are, insights into heaven granted to those on earth because God has "signaled" them (1:1).

In the prophetic tradition from which the Apocalypse draws, a sign is a perception that opens up the prospect of the divine realm to those who dwell in this world. For that reason, no sign, no vision, can be reduced to the conditions of the politics or circumstances of any passing moment. Rather, they await the witness of those who see the signs in their own terms, as invitations to join in the reality of God's power in heaven, and who are willing to use their lives to realize that righteousness on earth.

Further Reading

Leonard L. Thompson, *The Book of Revelation: Apocalypse and Empire* (Oxford: Oxford University Press, 1990); Bruce J. Malina, *On the Genre and Message of Revelation: Star Visions and Sky Journeys* (Peabody, Mass.: Hendrickson, 1995); James C. Vanderkam, *An Introduction to Early Judaism* (Grand Rapids: Eerdmans, 2001); John J. Collins, *The Apocalyptic Imagination: An Introduction to the Jewish Matrix of Christianity* (New York: Crossroad, 1984); R. H. Charles, *A Critical and Exegetical Commentary on the Revelation of St. John*, The International Critical Commentary (New York: Scribner's, 1920); Christopher R. Smith, "The Structure of the Book of Revelation in Light of Apocalyptic Literary Conventions," *Novum Testamentum* 36, no. 4 (1994): 373–93; J. L. Resseguie, *Revelation Unsealed: A Narrative Critical Approach to John's Apocalypse*, Biblical Interpretation Series 32 (Leiden: Brill, 1998); Stanley E. Porter, "The Language of the Apocalypse in Recent Discussion," *New Testament Studies* 35 (1989): 582–603; Elisabeth Schüssler Fiorenza, *The Book of Revelation: Justice and Judgment* (Philadelphia: Fortress, 1985); Lynn Huber, "Unveiling the Bride: Revelation 19:1-18 and Roman Social Discourse," in *A Feminist Companion to the Apocalypse of John*, ed. Amy-Jill Levine and Maria Mayo Robbins (London: T&T Clark, 2009), 159–79; Elaine Pagels, *Revelations: Visions, Prophecy, and Politics in the Book of Revelation* (New York: Viking, 2012); and Stefan Alkier, "Witness or Warrior? How the Book of Revelation Can Help Christians Live Their Political Lives," in *Revelation and the Politics of Apocalyptic Interpretation*, ed. Richard B. Hays and Stefan Alkier (Waco, Tex.: Baylor University Press, 2012), 125–41.

Notes

Introduction

1 Shaw's comment is contextualized in Loren L. Johns, *The Lamb Christology of the Apocalypse of John*, Wissenschaftliche Untersuchungen zum Neuen Testament 167 (Tübingen: Mohr, 2007), 4.

2 Translations of biblical and ancient texts are my own from the original Greek or Latin, unless otherwise noted.

Chapter 1

1 For description and analysis of the series and cinematic appropriations of the Apocalypse, see Bruce David Forbes and Jeanne Halgren Kilde, eds., *Rapture, Revelation, and the End Times: Exploring the Left Behind Series* (New York: Palgrave Macmillan, 2004); and Catherine Keller, *Apocalypse Now and Then: A Feminist Guide to the End of the World* (Boston: Beacon, 1996).

2 I have traced how this image emerged in Christianity and served as a model of conduct in *Abraham's Curse: Child Sacrifice in the Legacies of the West* (New York: Doubleday, 2008), 83–97.

3 Hierapolis is near Laodicea, one of the cities with a church addressed by the Revelation. Asia Minor is modern-day Turkey.

4 See William C. Weinrich, "The Image of the Wheat Stalk and the Vine Twig in the *Adversus Haereses* of Irenaeus of Lyons," *Concordia Theological Quarterly* 62, no. 3 (1998): 219–27.

5 See A. F. J. Klijn, "2 (Syriac Apocalypse of) Baruch," in *The Old Testament Pseudepigrapha* 1, ed. James H. Charlesworth (Garden City, N.Y.: Doubleday, 1983), 615–52. The millennial passage is 29:5-6.

6 See Gérard Vallée, *A Study in Anti-Gnostic Polemics: Irenaeus, Hippolytus, and Epiphanius*, Studies in Christianity and Judaism (Waterloo, Ont.: Wilfrid Laurier University Press, 1981), 9–40.

7 See Hermann Gunkel, *Creation and Chaos in the Primeval Era and the Eschaton,* translation of the 1895 German edition by K. William Whitney Jr. (Grand Rapids: Eerdmans, 2006), 239–47.

8 See Jacob M. Myers, *I and II Esdras: Introduction, Translation, and Commentary*, The Anchor Bible (Garden City, N.Y.: Doubleday, 1974); and Michael E. Stone, *Fourth Ezra* (Minneapolis: Fortress, 1990).

9 As is the Messiah in the *Psalms of Solomon* 7:27, a pseudepigraphical work from the first century BCE.

10 See Marcia L. Colish, *The Stoic Tradition from Antiquity to the Early Middle Ages*, vol. 1, Studies in the History of Christian Thought 34 (Leiden: Brill, 1985), 24–30.

11 Stoics sometimes associated afterlife with the permanence of the moon, following the myth of Endymion and Selene (the moon goddess). See Aristoula Georgiadou and David H. J. Larmour, *Lucian's Science Fiction Novel "True Histories": Interpretation and Commentary*, Mnemosyne, Bibliotheca Classica Batava Supplementum 179 (Leiden: Brill, 1998), 85.

12 J. H. Waszink, *Tertullianus, De Anima* (Turnhout, Belgium: Brepolis, 2010); and Edwin A. Quain, *Tertullian on the Soul*, Fathers of the Church (New York: Fathers of the Church, 1950). Tertullian makes the same argument in *On the Resurrection of the Flesh* 25 and 38.

13 Jean Daniélou, "La typologie millénariste de la semaine dans le christianisme primitif," *Vigiliae Christianae* 2 (1948): 1–16. The author shows that the *Book of Jubilees*, a Jewish pseudepigraphical work from the third century BCE, and *Second Enoch*, from late in the first century, helped shape the approach of the later Christian thinkers such as Justin and Irenaeus. Daniélou argues that the scheme was incorporated into Christian millenarianism by the time of the *Epistle of Barnabas* (15.3-8) in the second century. See also Justin, *Dialogue* 80.5; and Irenaeus, *Against Heresies* 5.28.3.

14 See T. C. Schmidt, *Hippolytus of Rome: Commentary on Daniel* (Chronicon.net, 2010).

Chapter 2

1 See Leif Carlsson, *Round Trips to Heaven: Otherworldly Travelers in Early Judaism and Christianity*, Lund Studies in History of Religions 19 (Stockholm: Almqvist & Wiksell, 2004). He particularly focuses on *1 Enoch* 14:8–16:3, 70:1–71:17; *2 Enoch*; *Testament of Levi* 2–5; the *Apocalypse of Zephaniah*; the *Apocalypse of Abraham*; the *Martyrdom and Ascension of Isaiah*; 2 Corinthians 12:1-5; Adam in the Latin and Greek versions of the *Life of Adam and Eve*; and *3 Baruch*.

2 This is the point of departure for Elaine Pagels, *Revelations: Visions, Prophecy, and Politics in the Book of Revelation* (New York: Viking, 2012). See James M. Robinson, ed., *The Nag Hammadi Library in English* (San Francisco: Harper & Row, 1978). This is the most widely used translation of the ancient library of gnostic books discovered in Egypt in 1945, and it also includes *The Gospel according to Mary*.

3 Joseph F. T. Kelly, "Early Medieval Evidence for Twelve Homilies by Origen on the Apocalypse," *Vigiliae Christianae* 39, no. 3 (1985): 273–79; and William

C. Weinrich, *Revelation*, Ancient Christian Commentary on Scripture: New Testament 12 (Downers Grove, Ill.: InterVarsity, 2005), xxi.

4 See S. R. F. Price, *Rituals and Power: The Roman Imperial Cult in Asia Minor* (Cambridge: Cambridge University Press, 1984), 1–11.

5 *Pantokrator* appears in Rev 1:8 in a way that might apply to God or to Christ, and then in 4:8; 11:17; 15:3; 16:7, 14; 19:6, 15; and 22:22, directed to God on the throne with which the Lamb is associated. Apart from one usage of *pantokrator* in Paul's letters to refer to God (2 Cor 6:18), the Revelation's nine occurrences dominate in the New Testament.

6 See Scott Hahn, *The Lamb's Supper: The Mass as Heaven on Earth* (New York: Doubleday, 1999), 9–76; and Massey H. Shepherd, *The Paschal Liturgy and the Apocalypse* (Richmond, Va.: John Knox, 1960), 77–87.

7 See Lactantius, *De mortibus persecutorum* 5.5, trans. Mary Francis McDonald in *Lactantius: The Minor Works*, Fathers of the Church 54 (Washington, D.C.: Catholic University of America, 1965), 142.

8 See Paula Fredriksen, "Apocalypse and Redemption in Early Christianity: From John of Patmos to Augustine of Hippo," *Vigiliae Christianae* 45, no. 2 (1991): 151–83, 157–60. (In the notes throughout this book, when there are two sets of page numbers, the first represent the whole article and the second the relevant pages.)

9 Jean Daniélou, "La typologie millénariste de la semaine dans le christianisme primitif," *Vigiliae Christianae* 2 (1948): 1–16, 16.

Chapter 3

1 See Ann Storey, "A Theophany of the Feminine: Hildegard of Bingen, Elisabeth of Schönau, and Herrad of Landsberg," *Woman's Art Journal* 19, no. 1 (1998): 16–20; and Barbara Newman, ed., *Voice of the Living Light: Hildegard of Bingen and Her World* (Berkeley: University of California Press, 1998), 52–69.

2 The context of the interview is nicely rendered in James Reston, *Warriors of God: Richard the Lionheart and Saladin in the Third Crusade* (New York: Doubleday, 2001), 136–37. See *The Annals of Roger de Hoveden*, trans. Henry T. Riley, vol. 2 (London: Bohn, 1853), 177–80.

3 See Alexander Roberts et al., *Ante-Nicene Fathers*, vol. 5 (Peabody: Hendrickson, 1994), 204–19.

4 This translation from the *Book of Figures* xiv, 9–55, appears in Bernard McGinn, *Visions of the End: Apocalyptic Traditions in the Middle Ages* (New York: Columbia University Press, 1979), 138.

5 See Marjorie Reeves, "Joachim of Fiore and the Images of the Apocalypse according to St. John," *Journal of the Warburg and Courtauld Institutes* 64 (2001): 281–95, 292.

6 This scenario from the *Harmony* is beautifully epitomized by Reeves, *Joachim of Fiore & the Prophetic Future* (Stroud, U.K.: Sutton, 1999), 12–13, who offers it together with a fine explanation of the importance of Benedict and the Cistercians to Joachim. Notably, Elijah was present at the transfiguration along with Moses and Jesus; one might understand Joachim's analysis as an exegesis of his vision on Mount Tabor.

7 See Brian Murdoch, *The Medieval Popular Bible: Expansions of Genesis in the Middle Ages* (Cambridge: Brewer, 2003), 19–41.

8 See J. A. Giles, "Chronicle of Richard of Devizes," *Chronicles of the Crusades* (London: Bohn, 1848), §3.

9 2 Thessalonians is a pseudepigraphical work which Roger takes to be genuine. He also accepts a personified view of "what restrains," following the reading "the one who restrains" in the next verse. See Bruce Chilton and Deirdre Good, *Starting New Testament Study: Learning, Doing* (London: SPCK, 2009), 144.

10 Tertullian's position is developed in *On the Resurrection of the Flesh*, 24–25.

11 Chrysostom makes his case in *Homily Four on Second Thessalonians*; see Philip Schaff, ed., *Nicene and Post-Nicene Fathers* (Grand Rapids: Eerdmans, 2002), 526–32. He also refers to the exegesis that the participle, appearing in the neuter gender, must refer to the Holy Spirit, which is also neuter in Greek.

12 Jerzy Pysiak, "Philippe Auguste: Un roi de la fin des temps?" *Annales, Histoire, Sciences Sociales* 57, no. 5 (2002): 1165–90.

13 A process beautifully described, with particular reference to Otto of Friesing, in Pierre Racine, *Frédéric Barberousse (1152–1190)* (Paris: Perrin, 2009), 157–58, 413; cf. Marjorie Reeves, "The Development of Apocalyptic Attitudes: Medieval Attitudes," *The Apocalypse in English Renaissance Thought and Literature: Patterns, Antecedents, and Repercussions*, ed. C. A. Patrides and Joseph Wittreich (Ithaca, N.Y.: Cornell University Press, 1984), 47.

14 Bernard McGinn, *Apocalypticism in the Western Tradition*, Variorum Collected Studies Series 430 (Surrey, U.K.: Ashgate/Variorum, 1994), 3.269. McGinn articulates this shift: "From roughly 300 to about 1100 A.D., the images from the Apocalypse tended to be read primarily in a spiritual sense, that is, as symbols of the present life of the church and its members, and only secondarily and intermittently as prophecies of present events or those of the coming final crisis of history. From about 1100, however, there was a resurgence in historicizing and prophetic uses of the symbols."

15 *Revelations of the Pseudo-Methodius*, cited and discussed with reference to secondary literature in Bernard McGinn, "The End of the World and the Beginning of Christendom," in *Apocalypse Theory and the Ends of the World*, ed. Malcolm Bull (Oxford: Blackwell, 1993), 58–89, 77–79; and Paul J. Alexander, "The Medieval Legend of the Last Roman Emperor and Its Messianic Origin," *Journal of the Warburg and Courtauld Institutes* 41 (1978): 1–15.

16 For discussion, see Paul J. Alexander, *The Byzantine Apocalyptic Tradition*, ed. Dorothy deF. Abrahamse (Berkeley: University of California Press, 1985), 223–25.

17 See Bernd Janowski and Peter Stuhlmacher, eds., *The Suffering Servant: Isaiah 53 in Jewish and Christian Sources*, trans. Daniel P. Bailey (Grand Rapids: Eerdmans, 2004) 189-224. This role of the Isaiah Targum within rabbinic theology is further detailed in Bruce Chilton, *The Glory of Israel: The Theology and Provenience of the Isaiah Targum*, Journal for the Study of the Old Testament Supplement 23 (Sheffield: JSOT, 1982), 13–96.

18 See David Cook, "An Early Muslim Daniel Apocalypse," *Arabica* 49, no. 1

(2002): 55–96, esp. 58–60, 67–96. For further examples of the genre, see idem *Contemporary Muslim Apocalyptic Literature* (Syracuse, N.Y.: Syracuse University Press, 2005), 82.

19 This is traced by Sylvia Schein, *Gateway to the Heavenly City: Crusader Jerusalem and the Catholic West (1099–1187)* (Aldershot, U.K.: Ashgate, 2005), 17–19 through the work of Guibert de Nogent. She also discusses the description of Raimond of Aguilers (24), who uses the imagery of blood and bridles.

20 See Jacques Le Goff, *The Birth of Purgatory*, trans. Arthur Goldhammer (Chicago: University of Chicago Press, 1984).

Chapter 4

1 For Gerardo, see Joseph L. Baird, Giuseppe Baglivi, and John Robert Kane, eds., *The Chronicle of Salimbene de Adam*, Medieval and Renaissance Texts and Studies 40 (Binghamton, N.Y.: Medieval and Renaissance Texts and Studies, 1986), 228–29, 463–68. Also, for Origen's view in *Commentary on John* 1.39-40, see Judith L. Kovacs, Christopher Rowland, and Rebekah Callow, *Revelation: The Apocalypse of Jesus Christ*, Blackwell Bible Commentaries (Hoboken, N.J.: Wiley-Blackwell, 2004), 164.

2 Marjorie Reeves, "The Development of Apocalyptic Thought: Medieval Attitudes," in *The Apocalypse in English Renaissance Thought and Literature: Patterns, Antecedents and Repercussions*, ed. C. A. Patrides and Joseph Wittreich (Ithaca, N.Y.: Cornell University Press, 1984), 41–73, 51.

3 See David Burr, *The Persecution of Peter Olivi*, Transactions of the American Philosophical Society 66.5 (Philadelphia: American Philosophical Society, 1976), 69–75; and Ruth Kerstenberg-Gladstein, "The 'Third Reich': A Fifteenth-Century Polemic against Joachimism and Its Background," *Journal of the Warburg and Courtauld Institutes* 18, no. 3/4 (1955): 245–95.

4 See Philip D. W. Krey, *Nicholas of Lyra's Apocalypse Commentary*, Consortium for the Teaching of the Middle Ages Commentary Series (Kalamazoo: Western Michigan University, 1997), 11–23.

5 Mark Musa, *Dante Alighieri's Divine Comedy* (Bloomington: Indiana University Press, 1996, 2004), 1:179, 1835, 5:121.

6 Philip D. W. Krey and Peter D. S. Krey, *Luther's Spirituality*, Classics of Western Spirituality (New York: Paulist, 2007), 47.

7 Krey and Krey, *Luther's Spirituality*, 52.

8 Krey and Krey, *Luther's Spirituality*, 53–56.

9 See Andrew Colin Gow, *The Red Jews: Antisemitism in an Apocalyptic Age*, Studies in Medieval and Reformation Thought 55 (Leiden: Brill, 1995), 158–79.

10 Krey and Krey, *Luther's Spirituality*, 55.

11 Jaroslav Pelikan, "Some Uses of Apocalypse in Magisterial Reformers," in *The Apocalypse in English Renaissance Thought and Literature: Patterns, Antecedents, and Repercussions*, ed. C. A. Patrides and Joseph Wittreich (Ithaca, N.Y.: Cornell University Press, 1984), 74–92, 74.

12 E. G. Rupp and Benjamin Drewery, *Martin Luther: Documents of Modern History* (London: Edward Arnold, 1970), 121–26. For the same appeal as applied to the crusades and its impact on the development of the Muslim

understanding of *jihad*, see Bruce Chilton, *Abraham's Curse: Child Sacrifice in the Legacies of the West* (New York: Doubleday, 2008), 171–95. For a good general description of the complexities involved in understanding the sources of the Peasants' War, see Tom Scott, "The Peasants' War," in *A Companion to the Reformation World*, ed. R. Po-chia Hsia (Oxford: Blackwell, 2006), 56–69.

13 See Mark U. Edwards, "Luther's Polemical Controversies," in *The Cambridge Companion to Martin Luther*, ed. Donald K. McKim (Cambridge: Cambridge University Press, 2003), 192–205; and Reeves, *The Apocalypse*, 141–42.

14 Peter Matheson, "Thomas Müntzer's Vindication and Refutation: A Language for the Common People?" *The Sixteenth Century Journal* 20, no. 4 (1989): 603–15; see also 21, no. 2 (1990): 258.

15 Krey and Krey, *Luther's Spirituality*, 49–50.

16 Krey and Krey, *Luther's Spirituality*, 49–50.

17 See Winfried Vogel, "The Eschatological Theology of Martin Luther, Part 2: Luther's Exposition of Daniel and Revelation," *Andrews University Seminary Studies* 25, no. 2 (1987): 183–99, 192; and Leon McBeth, *English Baptist Literature on Religious Liberty to 1689* (New York: Arno, 1980), 206–8.

18 Krey and Krey, *Luther's Spirituality*, 53.

19 Krey and Krey, *Luther's Spirituality*, 53.

20 Krey and Krey, *Luther's Spirituality*, 54.

21 Krey and Krey, *Luther's Spirituality*, 50.

22 See Calvin's *Institutes of the Christian Religion* 3.25, cited in Robert G. Clouse, *The End of Days: Essential Selections from Apocalyptic Texts—Annotated & Explained*, ed. Robert G. Clouse (Woodstock, Vt.: SkyLight, 2007), 67; and Irena Backus, *Reformation Readings of the Apocalypse: Geneva, Zurich, and Wittenberg*, Oxford Studies in Historical Theology (New York: Oxford University Press, 2000) 135–38.

23 See Richard Bauckham, *Tudor Apocalypse: Sixteenth-Century Apocalypticism, Millennarianism, and the English Reformation from John Bale to John Foxe and Thomas Brightman* (Oxford: Sutton Courtenay Press, 1978), 70–73. Bauckham goes on to show how widely apocalyptic conceptions were disseminated during the English Reformation outside the realm of commentary and doctrine, in plays, poetry, and hymns.

24 Bernard McGinn, *Antichrist: Two Thousand Years of the Human Fascination with Evil* (San Francisco: Harper, 1994), 226–30.

25 See Robert Clouse, "The Apocalyptic Interpretation of Thomas Brightman and Joseph Mede," *Journal of the Evangelical Theological Society* 11, no. 4 (1968): 181–93, 184.

26 Bernard Capp, "The Political Dimension of Apocalyptic Thought," in *The Apocalypse in English Renaissance Thought and Literature: Patterns, Antecedents, and Repercussions*, ed. C. A. Patrides and Joseph Wittreich (Ithaca, N.Y.: Cornell University Press, 1984), 93–124, 100–101.

27 Clouse, "The Apocalyptic Interpretation," 186–87.

28 Jeffrey K. Jue, *Heaven Upon Earth: Joseph Mede (1586–1638) and the Legacy of Millenarianism* (Dordrecht: Springer, 2006), 78–79.

29 Frank Ephraim Talmage, "David Kimhi on the Messianic Age," in *Disputation*

and Dialogue: Readings in the Jewish-Christian Encounter (New York: Ktav, 1975), 74–81.

30 Jue, *Heaven Upon Earth*, 79.

31 Johannes van den Berg, "Continuity within a Changing Context: The Apocalyptic Thought of Joseph Mede and Henry More," *Religious Currents and Cross-Currents: Essays on Early Modern Protestantism*, Studies in the History of Christian Thought 95 (Leiden: Brill, 1999), 83–101.

32 Susan Hardman Moore, *Pilgrims: New World Settlers & the Call of Home* (New Haven, Conn.: Yale University Press, 2007), 78.

33 Entry for 13 October 1660, in *The Diary of Samuel Pepys*, ed. Richard Le Gallienne (New York: Modern Library, 2003).

Chapter 5

1 For an analytic treatment of this and other Puritan contributions, with a helpful discussion of James Ussher's place among them, see Crawford Gribbon, *The Puritan Millennium: Literature & Theology, 1550–1682* (Dublin: Four Courts, 2000).

2 Andrew Janiak, ed., *Newton, Philosophical Writings*, Cambridge Texts in the History of Philosophy (Cambridge: Cambridge University Press, 2004), 90.

3 Isaac Newton, *Observations upon the Prophecies of Daniel, and the Apocalypse of St. John* (London, 1733), part 2, chap. 1, 251–52.

4 Isaac Newton, "9" in "Rules for Interpreting the Words & Language in Scripture," (unpublished Yahuda manuscript 1.1, National Library of Israel, Jerusalem).

5 Isaac Newton, *Philosophia Naturalis Principia Mathematica*, 2nd ed. (Cambridge: Cotes, 1713) 3:547 (General Scholium to Proposition 42).

6 This and other vignettes from Newton's life are related and ably documented in Michael White, *Isaac Newton: The Last Sorcerer* (Reading, Mass.: Helix, 1997).

7 This theme is pursued in detail in Stephen D. Snobelen, "Isaac Newton, Heretic: The Strategies of a Nicodemite," *The British Journal for the History of Science* 32, no. 4 (1999): 381–419, 418.

8 Jonathan Kirsch, *A History of the End of the World* (New York: HarperCollins, 2006) 176.

9 William Paley, *Natural Theology; or, Evidence of the Existence and Attributes of the Deity, Collected from the Appearances of Nature*, Oxford World's Classics, ed. Matthew D. Eddy and David Knight (London: Oxford University Press, 2006), 7. (From the book's opening metaphor, which was not original, as the editors point out.)

10 Isaac Newton, *Observations upon the Prophecies of Daniel, and the Apocalypse of St. John* (London: 1733), part 2, chap. 1, 251–52.

11 See C. Marvin Pate, *Reading Revelation: A Comparison of Four Interpretive Translations of the Apocalypse* (Grand Rapids: Kregel, 2009).

12 Jonathan Edwards, "Notebook Misc. 547," *The Philosophy of Jonathan Edwards from His Private Notebooks*, ed. Harvey G. Townsend (Eugene: University of Oregon Press, 1955), 135.

13 Jonathan Edwards, "Notebook Misc. 547."

14 Edwards, *A History of the Work of Redemption*, The Works of Jonathan Edwards 9, ed. John F. Wilson (New Haven, Conn.: Yale University Press, 1989), 189, 351–52, 457–58. See Glenn R. Kreider, *Jonathan Edwards's Interpretation of Revelation 4:1–8:1* (Lanham, Md.: University Press of America, 2004).

15 Edwards, *The Great Awakening*, The Works of Jonathan Edwards 4, ed. C. C. Goen (New Haven, Conn.: Yale University Press, 1972), 353.

16 Edwards, "Of Being," in *Scientific and Philosophical Writings*, Works of Jonathan Edwards 6, ed. Wallace E. Anderson (New Haven, Conn.: Yale University Press, 1980), 207.

17 Edwards, "Images of Divine Things," in *Typological Writings*, Works of Jonathan Edwards 11, ed. Wallace E. Anderson and Mason L. Lawrence (New Haven, Conn.: Yale University Press, 1993), 57, 67. Originally published in 1737.

18 William Blake, *Milton*, in *The Complete Poetry and Prose of William Blake*, ed. David V. Erdman (Berkeley: University of California Press, 2008), 127, lines 28:62–63. Erdman dates the poem ca. 1810 on p. 806. He gives a helpful account of how Blake reworked his material, and therefore complicated dating his works.

19 Blake's reference to the interval of two hundred years picks up on the claim of Moses Lowman that keys the events of the Apocalypse to increments of that period; see Moses Lowman, *A Paraphrase and Notes on the Revelation of John*, 3rd ed. (London: Cadell, 1773), 271.

20 Blake, *Milton*, in *Complete Poetry and Prose*, lines 58–61.

21 Blake, "All Religions Are One," in *Complete Poetry and Prose,* 1–2. Dated 1788 on p. 790.

22 Blake, *Jerusalem*, in *Complete Poetry and Prose*, p. 231, chap. 3, after plate 77. Dated 1810–14 on p. 809.

23 Blake, *Jerusalem,* p. 231, chap. 3, after plate 77.

24 Blake, *Milton,* in *Complete Poetry and Prose*, p. 118, lines 22:61–23:2.

25 Blake, "Night the Ninth," in *Complete Poetry and Prose*, p. 391, lines 122.15-20. Dated to ca. 1796–1807 on p. 817.

26 Blake, *Milton*, in *Complete Poetry and Prose*, p. 231, lines 1.13–16.

27 Blake, *Jerusalem*, in *Complete Poetry and Prose*, p. 155, lines 12.30–31.

28 Blake, "To the Christians," *Jerusalem*, in *Complete Poetry and Prose*, p. 232, chap. 3, plate 77.

29 Blake, *Jerusalem*, in *Complete Poetry and Prose*, pp. 200–201, chap. 3, plate 52. For another usage, linked to the criticism of law that is also dealt with here, see Harold Fisch, *The Biblical Presence in Shakespeare, Milton, and Blake: A Comparative Study* (Oxford: Clarendon, 1999), 219.

30 Blake, *Jerusalem*, in *Complete Poetry and Prose*, p. 202, lines 52:17–28.

31 See David V. Erdman, *Blake: Prophet Against Empire: A Poet's Interpretation of the History of His Own Times* (Princeton, N.J.: Princeton University Press, 1969), 269.

32 See Immanuel Swedenborg, *The Last Judgment and Babylon Destroyed: All the*

Predictions in the Apocalypse are at This Day Fulfilled (West Chester, Pa.: Swedenborg Foundation, 1952), 1-74.

33 Blake, *Milton*, in *Complete Poetry and Prose*, p. 124, lines 27:1–2.

34 Blake, *Jerusalem*, in *Complete Poetry and Prose*, p. 196, lines 48:4–11.

35 For the significance of this work within Blake's corpus, see Jeanne Moskal, "Forgiveness, Love, and Pride in Blake's 'The Everlasting Gospel,'" *Religion & Literature* 20, no. 2 (1988): 19–39.

36 See John Woolman, *The Journal and Major Essays of John Woolman*, ed. Phillips P. Moulton (1971; repr., Richmond, Ind.: Friends United Press, 2007), 32.

37 Woolman, *The Journal and Major Essays*, 23.

38 Entry for 1720–1742, in Woolman, *Journal*, 32.

39 He also said, "I find more wisdom in these pages than in any other book written since the days of the apostles." Emerson's views are discussed in the introduction to Woolman, *Journal*, 3.

40 Entry for 1720–1742, in Woolman, *Journal*, 28–29.

41 "A Little Gate to God," in *Walter Rauschenbusch: Selected Writings*, Sources of American Spirituality, ed. Winthrop S. Hudson (New York: Paulist, 1984), 46–48, 46.

42 Helena Petrovna Blavatsky, *Isis Unveiled: A Master-Key to the Mysteries of Ancient and Modern Science and Theology* (New York: Bouton, 1891), 2:12–13.

43 Christina Rossetti, *The Face of the Deep: A Devotional Commentary on the Apocalypse* (London: SPCK, 1892), 309–11; and Frederick S. Roden, "Two 'Sisters in Wisdom': Hildegard of Bingen, Christina Rossetti, and Feminist Theology," in *Hildegard of Bingen: A Book of Essays*, ed. Maud Burnett McInerney (Turnhout: Brepolis, 1998), 227–53.

44 Walter Rauschenbusch, *Christianity and the Social Crisis* (London: Macmillan, 1908), 142.

45 Rauschenbusch, *Crisis*, 106–7, 112.

46 Willem A. Visser 't Hooft, *The Background of the Social Gospel in America* (St. Louis, Mo.: Bethany, 1963), 79–80, 89–101, 127–44.

Chapter 6

1 See lecture 1 in William Miller, *Evidence from Scripture and History of the Second Coming of Christ, About the Year 1843* (Boston: Joshua V. Himes, 1842).

2 The pamphlet, entitled "The True Midnight Cry," is reproduced in Francis D. Nichol, *The Midnight Cry: A Defense of the Character and Conduct of William Miller and the Millerites* (Washington: Review & Herald, 1944). See also his lecture 16 in Miller, *Evidence from Scripture*.

3 Nichol, *Midnight Cry*, 457–62.

4 See M. James Penton, *Apocalypse Delayed: The Story of Jehovah's Witnesses* (Toronto: University of Toronto Press, 1985). For a discussion of the dates and their later adjustments, see pp. 197–201.

5 See Winthrop S. Hudson, ed., *Walter Rauschenbusch: Selected Writings*, Sources of American Spirituality (New York: Paulist, 1984), 79–94, 84–87, 88–94.

6 See William Kelly, ed., *The Collected Writings of J. N. Darby*, vol. 2, Ecclesiastical no. 1 (Winschoten: H. L. Heijkoop, 1972), 124–30.

7 John Nelson Darby, *Notes on the Book of Revelation: To Assist Enquirers in Searching into That Book* (London: Central Tract, 1839), 39–51.
8 *Scofield Reference Bible* (New York: Oxford University Press, 1909), 1276.
9 Cyrus Scofield, foreword to Lewis Sperry Chafer, *Satan* (New York: Gospel Publishing House, 1909), iii.
10 Matthew Avery Sutton, *Aimee Semple McPherson and the Resurrection of Christian America* (Cambridge, Mass.: Harvard University Press, 2007), 41.
11 Sutton, *Aimee Semple McPherson*, 69–77.
12 Aimee Semple McPherson, *This Is That: Personal Experiences, Sermons, and Writings* (Los Angeles: Bridal Call, 1919), 515.
13 Hal Lindsey, *The Late, Great Planet Earth*, with C. C. Carlson (Grand Rapids: Zondervan, 1970).
14 Ronald Weinland, *2008—God's Final Witness* (Cincinnati, Ohio: the-end.com, 2006), 244.
15 Rockerick C. Meredith, *Who or What Is the Antichrist?* (Charlotte, N.C.: Living Church of God, 2008), 9.
16 Meredith, *Who or What Is the Antichrist?* 13.
17 Meredith, *Who or What Is the Antichrist?* 36.
18 Quoted from a broadcast of the 700 Club and from Robertson's *The Secret Kingdom* in Paul Boyer, *When Time Shall Be No More: Prophecy Belief in Modern American Culture* (Cambridge, Mass.: Belknap, 1992), 138.
19 Tim LaHaye and Jerry B. Jenkins, *Desecration: Antichrist Takes the Throne*, In the "Left Behind" series, #9 (Carol Stream, Ill.: Tyndale House, 2001), 413–17.
20 See Motti Inbari, *Jewish Fundamentalism and the Temple Mount: Who Will Build the Third Temple?* trans. Shaul Vardi (Albany: State University of New York Press, 2009), 34. Inbari cites an interview that appeared in *Or Chozer* 7 (1991), and then, on p. 37, Ariel's *Prayerbook for the Temple*, 524–26.
21 Inbari, *Jewish Fundamentalism*, 37.
22 See The Temple Institute, http://www.templeinstitute.org/main.htm, accessed February 9, 2013, and Israel Ariel, ed., *Carta's Illustrated Encyclopedia of the Holy Temple* (Philadelphia: Coronet, 2004).
23 "Challenge," Temple Mount Faithful, http://www.templemountfaithful.org/challeng.htm, accessed February 9, 2013.
24 Inbari, *Jewish Fundamentalism*, 92.
25 "Membership," The Temple Institute, http://www.templeinstitute.org/membership.htm; and "Donors Wall," The Temple Institute, http://www.templeinstitute.org/donors_wall.htm. Accessed February 9, 2013.
26 Alex Heard, *Apocalypse Pretty Soon: Travels in End-Time America* (New York: Norton, 1999), 62–103.
27 Citations from Abu al-Husayn Muslim, *Sahih* (Beirut: Dar Ahya al Turath al-Arabi, 1982).
28 See Jean-Pierre Filiu, *Apocalypse in Islam*, trans. M. B. DeBevoise (Berkeley: University of California Press, 2011), 108.
29 See SalafiTalk.net, http://www.salafitalk.net/st/viewmessages.cfm?Forum=6&Topic=1969, accessed February 9, 2013.

30 Hank Hanegraaff, *The Apocalypse Code: Find Out What the Bible Really Says About the End Times . . . and Why It Matters Today* (Nashville: Nelson, 2007), 59, 236.

31 Hanegraaff, *Apocalypse Code*, 20.

32 See, e.g., Gershom Gorenberg, *The End of Days: Fundamentalism and the Struggle for the Temple Mount* (New York: Free Press, 2000), 233–50.

33 David Hartman, *Israelis and the Jewish Tradition: An Ancient People Debating Its Future* (New Haven, Conn.: Yale University Press, 2000), xi.

Chapter 7

1 J. Massyngberde Ford, *Revelation*, The Anchor Bible (New York: Doubleday, 1975), 30–37.

2 Margaret Barker, *The Revelation of Jesus Christ: Which God Gave to Him to Show to His Servants What Must Soon Take Place (Revelation 1.1)* (Edinburgh: T&T Clark, 2000), 99–100.

Scripture Index

General Index